THE POWER OF WHY: WHY 21 MUSICIANS CREATED A PROGRAM

GLORY ST. GERMAIN

COPYRIGHT

Compiled By: Glory St. Germain

Edited By: Wendy H. Jones and Lisa McGrath

Cover Design By: Glory St. Germain

DEDICATION

To my mom, who taught me about NEPD (Never-Ending Professional Development) and inspired me to become an entrepreneur.

To my dad, who taught me about the magic of music and the discipline required to master the art of musicianship.

And to my husband, Ray, for supporting me through all of my crazy 'Lucy' ideas and encouraging me to chase my dreams.

CONTENTS

IMPOSTER

Shirley Wang

United States

When Glory St. Germain asked me to write a chapter on why I created programs, I felt oddly inadequate. Sharing my ideas or thoughts is not so difficult, I would even say I am good, if not great at it, but to share my why or my personal story is a different matter. The thought made me feel flustered and vulnerable. I wonder how many of you have felt similarly, especially when someone asked you to step up and write a chapter with the subject of *you*. I procrastinated as I stewed in whatever it was that I felt. Then the lightbulb came on. I realized all the programs I created were to help people, including myself, overcome the terrible feeling of imposter syndrome.

Before we go any further, let me tell you a bit about myself. My name is Shirley Wang, but I was born Wang Hsiao-Ling in Taipei, Taiwan. When I was fifteen, my family decided to take on the great adventure of Life in America. Overnight, I became Shirley. Growing up, my biggest aspiration was to be a professional writer. And here is a slight problem for Shirley at age fifteen: I knew very little English. Needless to say, becoming a writer looked like an impossible dream. Fortunately, I was gifted as a young musician. At age seventeen, I was exposed to classical vocal literature. I quickly and hopelessly fell in love with all of it, from grand operas to esoteric art songs. The storytelling, the human emotions, and the unbelievable opportunity to use words in such creative and colorful means opened my young soul in unimaginable ways. It was too late for me to be competitive as a serious concert pianist. As an impetuous teenager, I thought, go big or go home. The piano wasn't for me. But as fate would have it, a few voice teachers in Los Angeles discovered my singing voice and offered me pro bono lessons. After a few months of training, I was accepted by one of the top music schools, The University of Southern California, ranked number four, just below Juilliard. It felt like a miracle!

Instead of beaming with pride and celebrating, I couldn't shake the feeling that I was just lucky. Maybe they made a mistake? Compared to my peers who had worked hard for years before they were accepted by USC, I felt I had to hide my lack of experience and training as a singer, even though I started my music studies on the piano at age four and was the strongest sight singer in the entire school. Walking around the campus, I felt like an imposter, afraid to be found out. Many opportunities continued to come my way. Still, I felt undeserving and questioned myself constantly. My overwhelming sense of inadequacy made me ignore many offers and possibilities. Despite all these internal struggles, my professional career as a performer and an educator began before graduating. I made it all the way to Carnegie Hall as an operatic soprano by blood, sweat, and tears. Believe me, when you hear people say, "How do you get to Carnegie Hall?" "Practice, Practice, Practice!" It is not an exaggeration. But it was also not enough. Being a musician is *hard*. As a young artist, I was enrolled in programs that made me a better singer, a better performer, a better musician, and a better linguist. Most importantly, they shaped me as a person and gave me tenacity. Otherwise, I would've quit a long time ago.

As a beneficiary of programs that enhanced my abilities as an artist, I wanted to extend these experiences to fellow performers and, later, my students. Let's take a moment to talk about the difference between services and programs. A program is a plan, including multiple services with an intention around changes, goals, objectives, outcomes, and indicators to measure progress towards the desired results. It is a response to a need, problem, or issue. On the other hand, a service is a set of activities which is helpful to the recipients; it is not structured to create fundamental and profound changes even if changes subsequently occur. This is why I prefer to create programs over providing services. I am interested in serving a greater purpose.

Along the way, I started creating and managing training programs, festivals, and concert series for singers and young pianists like myself. I produced my first concert opera performance of Mozart's *Cosi fan Tutte* at age twenty-three. The journey was bumpy but worth every moment. I wanted to help others as well as myself to stay on the quest for a lifetime. For those chosen by the music, this is not a temporary affair. Becoming and continuing to be a performing artist is a very solitary and challenging pursuit. It is led by countless hours of practice and studies. Then there is the career; through it all, life still happens. It was of great significance for me to create a community where people can grow and share resources.

Simultaneously, I started working with younger children, beginners from age four and up. It has been very important for me at a personal level to create access to top-quality music education early on and to expose these young students to the understanding of excellence and form a loving connection with music. This became my mission. It is a privilege to help young children realize these concepts are not mutually exclusive as they start to discover their own relationship with music. I am aware very few of these students will pursue a career in music, but many can and will become lifelong music lovers and supporters. Most importantly, there are so many incredible life lessons one can get through a well-rounded, carefully crafted music program.

The results have been remarkable. It created confident young people who defined themselves by efforts and progress. In a supported environment, they have grown inner-strength, resilience, and the ability to work through challenges without giving up. We planted the seeds of growth-based vs. a fixed mindset from a very early age.

To help others overcome the inner voice that yells out, "Imposter," has been my most significant reason to create programs. May we all continue on this journey. I hear you.

Author Bio:

Shirley Wang is an operatic soprano and a pianist who has performed across the U.S., including at Carnegie Hall. She founded *Simple Gifts Music Studio*, which offers online voice, piano, music theory, and Chinese cultural language programs.

https://www.SimpleGiftsMusicStudio.com

STICKS AND STONES CAN BREAK YOUR BONES... BUT WORDS CAN BREAK YOUR SOUL

Shelagh McKibbon-U'Ren

Canada

"Why can't you play that?" "You played that wrong again." "That sounded horrible." "Why don't you understand this?"

How did your piano teacher make you feel? Do you remember the words they used? Were they encouraging or negative? Peggy O'Mara, author of *Natural Family Living*, wrote "The way we talk to our children becomes their inner voice."

My inner voice was created by a piano teacher who was herself taught that only perfection was good enough; anything less was failure. My teacher would get frustrated when I struggled with Sight Reading and Ear Training (which came naturally to her). I could never learn the way that she was trying to teach me. I thought there was something wrong with me because I could not do what she was telling me to do. No one believed that sometimes it physically hurt to practice and that there were times when the black dots on the page got all jumbled up.

There is a place in this world for teachers who focus on students who have that ability to be another Mozart, to perform at Carnegie Hall, or who can pick up a piece and play it perfectly. But not every student is mentally, emotionally, and/or physically able to be 'that type of student'.

I started teaching piano at thirteen. I tried to be the type of teacher who produced perfect students. After all, wasn't my self-worth as a teacher based upon the performance and examination results of my students? In my late twenties, I was diagnosed with depression, anxiety, panic attacks, and dyslexia. Eventually, I was also diagnosed with degenerative osteoarthritis. I remembered that motto from my childhood, "Sticks and stones may break my bones, but names will never hurt me." What a load of horse doo-doo.

During therapy, I realized the power of the words that I had grown up with – the echoes - and I listened to the names that I was calling myself. They were destroying me. To start healing, I had to change how I was teaching.

Ignacio Estrada wrote, "If a child can't learn the way we teach, maybe we should teach the way they learn." This blew my mind. Understanding learning styles and learning abilities became my passion. I do not like the term learning disabilities. My dyslexia blessed me with the ability to learn outside the box – to discover different ways that I could learn and memorize.

When Glory St. Germain asked me to become the editor for the Second Edition of the *Ultimate Music Theory Series*, that old "not good enough" echo was overwhelming. How could I edit when I struggled with words and numbers? Then I realized that there had to be other teachers and students who struggled too. This was an opportunity for me to ensure that the *Ultimate Music Theory Series* could work for all learning styles, including special needs.

So, I wrote, edited, and completed each page a dozen times. Was everything perfect? Nope. Right after the books were published, we created matching online Errata Pages to list all the little things that I missed. Sigh. I received emails from teachers around the world who pointed out these silly errors. I started to get lost in that echo from my childhood, "You are not good enough."

I came within an inch of quitting. Glory helped me understand that making a mistake was not the end of the world. Mistakes were just boo-boos, and we would fix them in the next round of printing. She showed me that I could take my mistakes and turn them into teachable moments to educate others about learning styles and abilities.

It was time to turn my 'not good enough', my disabilities, into my superpowers.

I began to change my reaction in the studio when mistakes were made. I started explaining to my students and parents that I most definitely am going to make mistakes, especially with numbers and words. But instead of making fun of me, we are going to learn how to laugh *with* me rather than *at* me when I make mistakes.

Mistakes became less traumatic. When a student catches me writing page 24 instead of page 42, we actually say, in a sarcastic voice, "Oh no, the world is going to end because Mme. Shelagh wrote a 24 instead of a 42." Then we giggle at how silly we are being.

I know that my students are becoming less afraid of making mistakes when they can turn around and laugh at their own mistakes.

How we react to these mistakes can make the difference in a child believing in themselves instead of believing that they are not good enough. By teaching children to laugh *with* themselves, and not *at* themselves, we are teaching them important life skills.

Another change I needed to make was to change my words. In the past, when I thought that I had to be the perfect teacher of only perfect students, I would focus on fixing every mistake first before a piece was good enough for a compliment. After all, that was how I had been raised.

I stopped aiming for perfection (from myself and from my students). Yes, progress and playing correctly were important but praising came first.

When a child hears "Oh, wow, well done" or "nice dynamics" first, they feel confident. If they hear "Why didn't you play legato?" They feel disappointed in themselves.

For many of my students, I discovered that if I turned that constructive criticism into a challenge, they wanted to fix it!

I now say, "How about a challenge? This is going to be tricky, and you may feel like throwing your piano in the river, but I know that you can play those measures legato. You've played legato before, so I know that you can do it."

We then discuss strategies for what to do if it really becomes too tricky. Do we practice it hand separately? Do we play it super slowly? Do we close the book and play something else? Do we try again tomorrow?

By planning ahead for a difficult situation, we empower the student and give them confidence. Game changer!

You have the power to turn your disability into your superpower. If you are not happy being the teacher that you are, then change! If the echoes from your childhood have left you feeling low, then rewrite the script that you hear in your heart. You are *good enough*. Why not use your superpower?

Author Bio:

Shelagh McKibbon-U'Ren is the author of the *Ultimate Music Theory Exam Series*, and the *Examiner for the Ultimate Music Theory Certification Course*. She continues to educate Teachers through her UMT Blogs and Coaching Calls. But her favorite role is "Maw-Maw" to her grandchildren.

https://UltimateMusicTheory.com

BREAKING THROUGH THE TALENT MYTH

Christopher Sutton

United Kingdom

"Whoa... why did nobody ever tell me about this?!"

I was stunned... confused... and extremely excited.

As I stood there with fingers tingling, my brain was on fire. I felt more alive than I had in years. It was like the world had just cracked open and a vast new landscape had opened up in front of me.

This was back in 2008, and I had done something incredible: I had played *Mary Had a Little Lamb* on the piano.

Now that may not seem like a big deal, especially considering I had over fifteen years of musical training behind me and played several instruments. But I had played it entirely by ear, no sheet music in sight, after years of thinking playing by ear was something only talented, gifted, natural musicians could do. Now, suddenly, it seemed like everything I had taken as a fact about my own musical abilities and potential was turned upside-down.

My first thought was, "Oh my gosh, did I really just do that?" But as the shock and surprise wore off, and I spent more time exploring this new ability, my excitement turned into a new kind of frustration: in a decade and a half of music lessons, why had nobody ever told me this was possible for me?

I had learned music from a young age, with singing classes and playing the recorder, and since I went to a school with a strong music department and I loved music, I naturally moved on to more and more musical activities.

I learned cello, clarinet, saxophone, then guitar and piano. I sang in church choirs, barbershop groups, and musicals. I performed, solo and in ensembles, in informal gigs, formal concerts in large auditoriums, and on theatre stages. I took lessons, practiced, and passed my instrument exams up to Grade 8 with top marks.

On paper I was a very good musician - one of the best in my year group. I was known as 'the musical one' in my class.

But here's the thing: I never felt musical. Not really.

In fact, I always felt like a fraud. An imposter. Someone who was just playing at being a musician.

While I struggled and pretended, I would see other musicians for whom it all seemed to come easily. Not only could they do what I could better, faster, and easier - they could do things I could only dream of.

Play by ear. Improvise. Compose. Arrange. Collaborate and jam with confidence.

It seemed like magic. I had absolutely no idea how they did it. When I tried it myself, I fell flat on my face. So, I concluded they must just be different.

They were the *real* musicians. They clearly had a talent, a gift, a natural ability in music that I just did not have.

Or so I thought.

Year by year I struggled away, despite feeling like it was all somewhat pointless because I'd never be a *real* musician.

Then in 2008, everything changed.

As part of my day job, I was introduced to something called 'golden ears' training for studio engineers, and as I explored that I stumbled into the related area of 'musical ear training'.

My mind was blown.

For years I had taken grade exams with an aural skills component where I would be tested on things like recognising intervals by ear. And for years, this had seemed like just another part of talent. Some bits I could do, others I had absolutely no clue about.

Now as I explored 'ear training', I discovered a whole world of music learning I had never encountered before, a world which promised to actually teach me the skills I thought were magic.

In fact, as I dug into it, I discovered that the scientific research had already proven conclusively that talent is a myth, and every single ability we associate with musical talent is, in fact, learnable.

I put aside my old limiting beliefs and started to apply these ear training methods, and I soon found myself able to play by ear and improvise - starting simply with *Mary Had a Little Lamb* but quickly progressing to levels I'd never dreamed of.

What's more, I realised there was something even more powerful happening: I was starting to actually feel like a *real* musician.

My excitement combined with sheer astonishment that this incredible treasure had been hidden in plain sight all those years, and I found myself itching to do something to save others from the years of struggle, frustration, and disappointment I'd gone through myself.

So even though I'd never expected or intended to start a business, I founded my company in 2009 with the goal of making this kind of musicality training so easy, fun, and effective that it would spread like wildfire among music learners and deliver them the kinds of concrete new abilities and deep identity shifts that I had experienced so powerfully myself.

Now, I'm not going to pretend it's been an easy journey since then. I had a huge amount to learn about business, marketing, and indeed the whole topic of musicality itself. But we're blessed to live in an age when the world's knowledge is at our fingertips and help is always just an email away. From the beginning I was able to hire music educators more expert than myself to contribute to the project and grow something vastly bigger and better than I ever could have done alone.

I'm proud to say that we now reach over 100,000 musicians every month through our website, podcast, and apps. We have the honour of serving over 10,000 members in our online training program, *Musical U*, with a team of some of the most expert and devoted music educators in the world.

Every day I have the thrill of hearing of insights and aha moments shared by our students inside *Musical U*, and each time I hear someone say, "Oh my gosh, I never knew I could do that," or "Why did nobody tell me about this?" I know we're doing our part to build a better future for all music learners.

I was never formally trained as a music teacher or entrepreneur, and I look nothing like you might expect the leader of a music education company to - but there's no doubt in my mind that this was what I was put on this planet to do. I am deeply proud of how far we've come and excited for what comes next. That's just what finding and following your why can do for you.

Author Bio:

Christopher Sutton is the founder of *Musical U*, the world's leading provider of online musicality training, specialising in adult music learners. He lives in London with his wife, two daughters, and far too many instruments.

https://www.musical-u.com/

TURNING CLOSET SINGERS INTO CONFIDENT SINGERS

Benny Ng

Australia

On the courtyard of the University of Sydney, students and lecturers alike walked at various paces under the scorching afternoon sun.

I stood in the middle of it with a stack of flyers in my arms.

It was the beginning of my vocal coaching career. I was handing out flyers in the hopes of recruiting my first students.

You Can Sing! the flyers said.

When people saw the flyers, some of them would laugh and some of them would scoff: "Me? Singing? Not a chance…"

I was perplexed. I always thought the voice was an instrument we could learn to 'play'.

I was determined to change this paradigm. I wanted to prove to aspiring singers that they were wrong about themselves.

I wanted to prove to them that they could sing.

You see, I have always loved singing.

Coming home from school, I would blast music on the computer speakers and belt out my favorite songs.

I could sing (mostly) in tune and in time but a good tone was elusive. Although I had a high voice, I found it difficult to sing high notes without yelling or feeling 'stuck' in my throat.

I started taking singing lessons when I was seventeen, but singing was still such a mystery to me.

As someone who loved details, I found it hard to accept something without understanding the inner workings of it.

No disrespect to the teachers I had during that time, but none of them gave me a complete picture of how the voice worked. I was shown bits and pieces and had gaps in my knowledge. As a result, my progress in singing slowed to a crawl.

I realized that if I did not do something about that I would never become a professional singer. So, I enrolled in the Sydney Conservatorium of Music.

It was there that I discovered the things that I had always wanted to know about the voice. Darkness dissipated as I was enlightened by the lectures and research sessions in the library.

The open throat concept revealed itself to me as the foundation of vocal technique. It would eventually become the cornerstone of my teachings.

My journey towards becoming the singer that I am today was arduous. I had to overcome roadblocks after obstacles, before gaining control of my voice.

That is why I wanted to make it easier for other aspiring singers. I wanted them to intellectually understand how the voice works, develop awareness and muscle memory of vocal techniques, then apply them while singing songs.

No more stumbling in the dark.

Singing is such a rewarding thing to do but it is also quite abstract. I mean, how can you play an instrument that you cannot see or touch? Imagine playing the piano in the dark while standing five feet away from it...

I wanted to take the guesswork out of learning to sing.

Over the past ten years, I have worked with singers of different genres and ability levels. I planned every lesson that I taught and fine-tuned my pedagogy to get the best results for my students. A syllabus was inadvertently developed.

As my experience grew, so did the quality of my lessons. The AHA moments my students got every time we achieved a breakthrough were the highlight of my lessons. It was such a rewarding feeling - knowing the techniques that I taught were changing people's lives through instilling confidence in their voice.

The gratitude on their faces motivated me to keep providing value to my students.

I knew I had to do everything in my power to get this material out to as many people as possible.

It was January 2019. I was on an eight-hour plane trip to Malaysia. On the plane, I came up with my business name: *Top Singing Secrets*. I created a draft for an online singing academy.

It was not until eight months later that my plans would actualize.

An email titled: *Looking for Artists and Entrepreneurs* popped into my inbox. It was sent by Michael Elsner from *Master Music Licensing*. It was an invitation to join his *Business Building Bootcamp*.

I applied and was over the moon when Michael told me my application was successful. The purpose of the bootcamp was to build and launch an online business from scratch in the space of nine weeks.

A steep learning curve and late nights ensued. I studied the required readings, built my website and finished my online singing academy using a platform called Kajabi.

In December 2019, *Singing Confidence Academy* was launched, and I made over $1,000 in sales that month.

Although it was not an astronomical amount, it was an important milestone for me as a digital entrepreneur.

Stoked by the positive transformation I saw in the students who enrolled, the fire in my belly is stronger than ever.

Now, I help singers from all over the world become proud of their voice without risking embarrassment or judgment - anytime, anywhere.

The fact that I can achieve that without the limitations of time and location is extremely satisfying and liberating.

As musicians, we impact the world through the power of our music that is played on wide-reaching platforms (e.g. radio, TV, YouTube, online streaming services).

Why not do the same as music teachers? Why not spread our teachings to as many people as we can, in as little time as possible?

The technology is here. We just need to make use of it. The future of young aspiring musicians is in your hands.

What are you going to do about it... and why?

Author Bio:

Benny Ng is a vocalist/songwriter of *Shadowary* (melodic rock band) and founder of *Top Singing Secrets*. He helps people gain control of their voice and become confident singers.

https://www.topsingingsecrets.com/

HOW I DISCOVERED MUSIC MENTORING IS MY MOJO

Susan Niekamp

United States

My life's aha moment presented itself in 3rd grade. It was then that I realized I wanted to be a music teacher and so began a lifelong journey of mentoring music students.

When I was in elementary school, I went home every day and lined up all my stuffed animals and dolls into neat rows in front of my large chalkboard. I spent hours teaching my homework to the wide-eyed, inanimate students using large, colored, sidewalk-chalk for different subjects. I walked among my students, asking who needed help as I went. I developed my teaching skills. When lessons were finished for the day, we would have our music time. I put on my favorite Olivia Newton-John record, held my marker in my hand as a microphone, stood on my pretend stage, and sang.

From kindergarten through 8th grade, music was my life. My days were filled with choir rehearsals and private lessons for piano, voice, and clarinet. I attended a small private school where I participated in many diverse activities, but with only thirteen students in my class, we had to combine grades just to create sports teams. In addition to music, I was involved in basketball, volleyball, softball, track, cheerleading, student council, and drama club. I was very competitive and driven to prove others wrong if they doubted my passions, dreams, or desires.

Since my school didn't have enough students to make a band, I was bussed each week to the nearby junior high school to play in concert and jazz bands. I remember my parents nagging me to turn off the TV and do something productive. I didn't appreciate it at the time, but I dutifully practiced singing and playing the clarinet and piano every day. However, I struggled with music theory concepts, scales, and key signatures. I found myself in tears many afternoons, all while preparing for All State and solo competitions. To make matters worse, my music teachers were neither motivating nor fun. I felt buried in advanced music theory concepts with minimal instruction. Fortunately, frustration turned into determination. I knew I had some talent and a good ear, but I also knew what was lacking: direction. If someone wasn't going to help me, I would figure it out myself.

My determination paid off. In high school, I earned first chair clarinet in both band and orchestra, I swirled across the field as drum major of the marching band and became president of the school choir and show choir. These accomplishments came with parental support and many hours of dedicated practice; yet, with all the high fives and smiles came the realization that my mojo was beginning to wane because I never really understood music theory. When a new band director arrived and gave us a written music theory exam, I nearly failed it. I was devastated! How could I accomplish so many things in music and not really have a clue?

I had flashbacks to a stern private lesson teacher who handed me 'The Circle of 5ths' and commanded me to memorize it. The frustration and doubt returned. I begged my parents to let me quit the band. I sought ways to avoid the anguish of it all. I even secretly recorded myself practicing. I played the recording over and over until my required practice time finally came to an end. Eventually, guilt set in, for I knew I was only fooling myself.

Then came the epiphany I desperately needed.

I thought back to the days of teaching my stuffed animals and dolls. I knew the teacher was supposed to know more than her students, so I began teaching private piano, voice, and clarinet lessons. I discovered I was good at breaking down large concepts into bite-sized pieces. As I explained concepts to students, I pieced together the mysteries of music theory until it all made sense. I had turned a corner.

The next pivotal chapter of my life was taking the SAT to get into college. I also had to audition in both voice and clarinet in front of a panel of music professors to gain admittance. There was a period of nail-biting agony, and for a short time, I felt overwhelmed and cried more than once. Once again though, I dug deep inside myself to figure out what to do. I made a list of past struggles and all the misguided, negative comments from the past. Then I made a second list that included my goals and an action plan to offset the negativity and prove people wrong. That did the trick. I was going to college!

I went on to earn a Bachelors in Music Education with a K-12 teaching certification, and I eventually accomplished a dream of having my own private music studio in Fort Myers, Florida. I kept a promise to myself that I would never allow any student to cry over 'The Circle of 5ths' or anything else he or she didn't understand. I created dozens of games with manipulatives and teaching strategies to help students understand the language of music.

I have learned how to make a difference in my students' lives and give them confidence to overcome fears, stage fright, and rejection. The TV is still off in my house as I continue to learn and challenge myself to be a better mentor for my students. It is important that my students don't experience doubts or negativity. My studio is a safe place where students can take risks and push boundaries without fear.

If you feel you've lost the music mojo in your life, let's get it back. Let me share ways to engage and inspire yourself and your students. I published a paper called *Play-dough + Popsicle Sticks + Paper Plates = Music Theory? Maybe it can help you.*

I challenge you to write your goals and spend time in activities that produce long-term benefits. Inspire yourself to fill your music education toolbox with new strategies. Surround yourself with positive people and keep the focus on your passions, dreams, and desires.

My mission is to help people of all ages and abilities unleash their creative potential and express themselves through music, the language of emotion. My studio provides a safe and comfortable environment that allows students the freedom to take risks, grow, have fun, and flourish!

What is your mission as an educator? And what's your why?

Author Bio:

Susan Niekamp is a vocal specialist who inspires students to optimize their talents. Her students have performed at Carnegie Hall, The Sydney Opera House, and have sung back-ups for Kristen Chenoweth and Barry Manilow.

https://susan-niekamp.squarespace.com/

MUSIC IN A CHILD'S WORLD

Frances Balodis

Canada

The most powerful statement, made to me on March 6, 1980, was "How many pianos and organs have you sold as a direct result of your lessons?" I knew at that moment that I would leave the commercial program in which I was successfully involved and develop another avenue to share the gift of music with children and adults.

I was not interested in any commercial aspect and had the motivation to create a program that was not associated with any commercial product.

We had two young children in 1980, ages 5 ½ and 3 ½, and I wanted both of these children to have their lives enriched with music – and I wanted them to enjoy the music journey.

I became a Registered Music Teacher in 1974 (ARCT Teachers) and have a Masters in Special Education from Acadia University (1972) plus I have been teaching music since 1958, so I knew I had the education and the experience to write a music program. My husband really convinced me that I could do it.

It wasn't easy at that time to write a music program as the music notation had to be written by hand. All music notation at that time was sent to the Far East to be put on metal plates for printing. This wasn't going to happen, so I wrote the notation by hand.

I wanted the program to be using all channels of learning – sight, hearing, tactile, and kinesthetic – plus logic. I had studied these channels and knew that everyone has their own unique learning style that is supported by the other channels. So, this required that I find an artist to illustrate the keyboard section and the singing section. We all love illustrations.

The people that were enrolled in the commercial program I was teaching were very supportive of switching to a program of my own design. One parent, who came to learn more about the commercial program said that he would support a program of my own design; he trusted me to do the best for his children.

A tin sheet with a grand staff on one side and a keyboard on the other was a great kinesthetic tool. I went to a metal shop, walked around, chose the grade of metal for this learning tool, and chose the correct size. Then we had to find magnets which we punched out by hand from rolls of magnetic strip. One has to be creative and focused to manipulate raw materials into learning tools.

The program was multi-leveled. Children could begin at any age. The levels all led to the graduating level which contained material from the Royal Conservatory of Music Grade One. This was important as music from that institution was recognized by private teachers. When someone graduated from my program, they could continue in private lessons, and the teacher would know and understand what level they had previously completed. The multi-level approach was important for some children in the program. If a child was a weak student at one level and was not quite ready to go to the next level, they could transition to a mid-level which would provide reinforcement and move them ahead gradually. This happened to many children in the program, some of whom have now gone on to complete Master's degrees at McGill.

The aspect of group was important to me - up to 6 children and parents in a group - because I knew the children would find it fun to be with others their own age and would learn from other children's questions and challenges. They would also be motivated by others.

The importance of a parent attending the music class was important to me. The parent would hear how the concept was taught, for example why we were learning about a fireman, and why the concept was taught in a certain manner, and what was expected at home. The parent could also be responsible for finding pages in the multi-unit book each child had - Ensembles, Homework, Keyboard, Listening, Singing and Warmups. The partnership of child-parent-teacher was extremely important.

The concept of 'inch by inch, life's a cinch, by the yard life is hard' is evident in this music program. The learning steps are small, thus more success is achieved. This is important to me as the dropout rate of students in private lessons is very high, due to frustration. In this music program I wanted students to feel success, and the dropout rate is extremely low.

I wanted to name each of the white keys on the piano as friendly characters to which the students could relate. These characters are fun friends about which to sing and fun friends to hold in puppets. These characters become very real to the children, and I was looking for a child-friendly approach.

The characters for each of the note values were important because the grown-up idea of counting is foreign to young children. Thus the "slee-py pan-da, the tur-tle, the hop and the bus-y beav-er" worked well for the "great big whole note, the half note, the quarter note and the eighth note".

Thinking about the importance of the auditory learning channel, the Listening section of the book provided opportunities for listening for rhythm patterns, dynamics, melodic patterns, tempo introduction and changes.

Solfege was introduced with hand signs and arm signs – good for singing, good for visual clues, and good for kinesthetic learning.

So, the all-round presentation of a music education was important to me in the formation of *Music for Young Children*. Using all the learning channels and appealing to the various personality types of dominant, interactive, sensitive, and cautious was important to me and remains steadfast in the MYC (myc.com) program 40 years later.

If you are thinking of writing or forming a program, I suggest you give much thought to the long-journey and not the flash-in-the-pan success. This will ensure that as the creator you feel your contribution is worthy, time-honoured and will stand the test of time.

Author Bio:

Frances Mae Balodis MEd., ARCT, LCCN(H), LCNCM(H), RMT, MYCC is founder (in 1980) of *Music for Young Children*® and cofounder of *CLU*™, certified NLP and an Accredited DISC Training provider.

https://www.myc.com/

OUT OF THE STRONG CAME FORTH SWEETNESS

Rami Bar-Niv

Israel/USA

In 1996 I was one of the pioneers who joined the computer and Internet revolution. Though still in the early days of the Internet, it changed my professional and personal life: contact with people all over the world became so much easier and faster, mass communication was available, I joined music and piano groups that enriched my connections, and many new opportunities emerged. Among the various opportunities to give concerts, adjudicate, lecture, and teach, there was an offer that I accepted: to teach, perform, and give master classes at a piano camp for adults in Vermont, USA. I made lots of new friends at camp and many of them invited me to their parts of the country and their parts of the world to teach and give concerts. I loved doing it all and did it a few times a year for about ten years, until one day I was fired.

But, as in Samson's riddle (Judges, Chapter 14:14), "Out of the

Strong Came Forth Sweetness". During my ten years at the piano camp in Vermont, some people tried to organize and create their own piano camps for adults in various places in the United States. They were mostly unsuccessful. In those years it never occurred to me to do my own piano camp. I was happy being employed and not having the extra responsibilities of owning and running a camp. However, after I was fired it seemed the natural thing to do, and I had quite a following. It didn't take me long to realize that I could actually create my own piano camp for adults, and I did. Of course, it helped that I had past experience in management and organization of concerts, concert series, piano studio, and festivals. There was only one problem, I didn't have a venue for camp.

Since 1996 I've also been going to Utica, NY to teach and give concerts. I acquired many friends in Utica too, and when the time came, they helped me explore various premises for a camp. Mary Murphy, a piano teacher and friend, drove me around exploring music stores and accommodation possibilities for the campers. Sharon Wagner, a piano teacher who along with her mother Clare had already adopted me as a family member in 1997, drove me around exploring music studios and churches. Sar-Shalom Strong, a concert pianist and teacher, helped me explore the music departments of the colleges in Utica.

The opus 1 Rami's Rhapsody Piano Camp for Adults took place in November 2006 at the Wagners' home in Clinton, New York – a suburb of Utica. The Wagners had three pianos in three different rooms, and that was sufficient for six participants taking turns practicing in two shifts. Clare cooked breakfast and lunch for us, and for dinner we went out or brought in take-outs. We also did some group activities in other venues: we held master classes at the beautiful home of Anne DeLia and held camp recitals on the beautiful Steinway grand at Mary Murphy's home. Later on, we also held camp recitals at Ann's and at the piano store, Center Stage Pianos. Nowadays, Anne also has at her home a beautiful Steinway grand that I helped her choose.

Actually, we have developed a sort of a tradition that camp's opening night is a party at Anne DeLia's place.

Camp spread, and I created and ran branches in Barbados, New Zealand, Washington D.C., and San Francisco. After a few years at the Wagners' home, camp moved to a church in Whitesboro – another suburb of Utica where Sharon was serving as organist and music minister. Actually, camp's move followed Sharon's pianos, as she had already moved two of her pianos into the Whitesboro Church.

After a few years at the church, camp moved into the piano store and the studios at Center Stage Pianos in New Hartford, yet another suburb of Utica.

I was fortunate and grateful that many of my pianist and musician friends came to perform at camp and to give master classes. To name just a few: pianists Sar-Shalom Strong, Tina Toglia, Benita Rose, Zitta Zohar, Anita Humer, organists Stephen Best and Bruce Smith, and soprano Anita Firman.

I do camp because I love teaching and sharing my knowledge with the students who are eager to learn. During the week of camp, each student gets five one-hour private-lessons. We have an opening night, evening master classes, and a closing recital on the last day of camp. The participants are adult amateurs of all levels, professional pianists, piano teachers, and composers. They come from all over the USA, Canada, and from all over the world. We also play duets and trios and often go to concerts together. Camp has catered to other instrumentalists and to singers, as well as to younger students in special designated master classes. In addition to all the learning, there are wonderful friendships that develop at camp and we all have lots of fun together.

Glory St. Germain, Founder/CEO of *Ultimate Music Theory* and the producer of this book series, interviewed my campers on one of her video broadcasts. That was a great way to hear their own versions of The Power of Why. Each of the campers told their story of piano playing, whether they played from childhood or started as adults being complete beginners, whether they were piano teachers, or composers. They come to camp because they love music and piano playing. They come to camp to enhance their piano playing, learn correct piano-playing techniques, get advice about composition and music notation, and engraving. They also rehabilitate from injuries and learn efficient fingering, interpretation guidelines, and styles of the various periods and composers. We discuss sight reading, memorization, and performance joy. We often have master classes and performances by other artists and masters. The master classes are a great opportunity for the campers to practice performing. The master classes also provide a great opportunity for learning to teach and to comment on other campers' performances; everyone gets to comment on the performances of the others. Above all is the love of music, friendship, and fun.

I created the camp program because I love it, because I love people, and I love sharing the glory of music and making music with others. I love seeing their progress and their joy of learning and playing the piano. They tell me I inspire them, but they are the ones who inspire me.

Who do you want to inspire with your music?

Author Bio:

Rami Bar-Niv, international pianist, composer, author, teacher. Born: Tel-Aviv, 1945. Graduated: Rubin Academy of Music, NYC's Mannes College of Music. Founded *Rami's Rhapsody Piano Camp*. Authored *The Art of Piano fingering, Blood, Sweat, and Tours*.

http://www.ybarniv.com/rami

MY MUSIC - MY SAVING GRACE

Heather Revell

New Zealand

It was the summer of 1971. She was thirteen years old. She was in swimming class. She loved hanging out in the pool with her classmates. Swimming was always fun. The water splashing her face, racing lengths of the pool with her friends. She felt free when she was in the pool. The whistle blew, and it was time to get out.

She raced back to the changing rooms even though they were not meant to run. While getting dressed, her friend mentioned she knew a secret. She wasn't sure if she should share it but after some coaxing, she did. And this is what she said. "I found out that you are adopted." And she proceeded to say that her parents had shared that information with her and said it was a secret.

BOOM! BOMBSHELL!

That was the day my world fell apart. I could not stand. I slumped to the floor. I could not think. My brain hurt, and my heart cracked into pieces. Questions flooded my hurting head. Who am I? What does this mean? Everyone knew this secret except me. I was alone. I was not wanted by my 'real' mother. How could someone throw me away? How could someone reject her baby? My life was a lie. My parents had lied to me.

I had a wonderful upbringing with extended family and friends galore. Long summers with my cousins at the beach house and riding horses on our farm. I was loved, safe, and supported. I had a wonderful big playroom filled with treasures. I spent many hours lining up my dolls and teddies and teaching them with my chalkboard and books.

I began piano lessons at the local convent when I was seven years old. And within a few short years was performing and competing on stages around my region. My mother and I would travel by bus or train to the city and buy beautiful dresses and shoes to perform in; I loved it. I had ribbons and trophies and awards. I loved playing piano and began singing and violin lessons when I was ten.

But in the summer of 1971, I was not so sure about my life anymore. I now knew my life was a lie. I had no one in this world. I had no true family. I felt totally alone. I withdrew from my family. I withdrew from my friends. I withdrew so much that I spent hours hiding under my bed, crying, fearful, and lonely.

Months after receiving that devastating news, I went out for a walk and didn't return home until three days later after the police found me. I was angry, hurt, and defensive for a few years. I wanted to hurt everyone, especially my parents. I did every stupid thing I could think of just to lash out.

When I thought no one was listening, I would go to the living room, shut the doors, and play my piano. Some days I would bash the notes in anger especially when playing Beethoven or Bach. I particularly disliked Bach, and I could feel some relief from my rejection by playing his fugues. I would rage and cry while I played. At other times, I played softer, more quietly, and poured my aching self into the piano. I found myself playing exactly what I felt. And most of those times, I didn't play any particular pieces. I poured my feelings into my piano as I improvised. The music soothed me and seemed to release my inner most sadness and confusion.

My music lessons continued through those tough years, and I had also started flute and guitar lessons. When I was fourteen, I was approached by the school Music Master. He asked me to learn the double bass so I could tour with the school orchestra to Fiji. I had four months to do it. He had heard through the grapevine that I was a good musician. The crazy thing was though, I had done my best to stay under his radar. My rejection and low self-worth had made me very wary of others.

Well, the trip to Fiji was a huge carrot and I went straight for it. It made me feel wanted. I had not felt that in such a long time. Yes, my parents had done their best to reassure me that they loved me and worked on bridging the gap, but I wouldn't have a bar of it. My need to lash out at anyone in my family or circle of friends was strong. I picked up the double bass with no problems and was off to Fiji with the school orchestra.

I started to teach piano when I was fifteen. I had passed my ABRSM Grade 6 practical and theory exams by then and wanted to teach young kids. I didn't really know anything about teaching, but I knew that I loved kids, and I loved playing piano. So, I advertised in the local rag and began teaching two sisters. And that is how my music teaching business began.

As my teaching program evolved over the years, this true passion became my sole driver along with my love of children and music. I continued my own lessons until I passed my ATCL when I was nineteen.

I loved teaching my students. It all boiled down to one basic strategy: creating a program that was fun. I created little songs for my students. We would play standing up or kneeling. We used our hands to create rain drops onto the piano. Sometimes we played with our eyes shut. We played duets. I loved teaching music to children.

To this day, when I experience ups and downs in my life, I sit at the piano and play out my feelings. I am so blessed to have this ability at my fingertips.

The rejection I felt as a teenager and the healing I received through my playing during those years, drove me to the one thing I love - a program of music. I connected my love for piano with teaching children and found my saving grace.

Author Bio:

Heather Revell is passionate about teaching music to children. She shares her passion and insight with music teachers and students through her online mentoring program and teaching business.

https://musicwithheather.com/

SHOULD I DO IT? WHY NOT?

Joanne Barker

Canada

Have you ever made a decision that you know could change things for the better and suddenly found yourself in a life-threatening situation? I have. One of the biggest decisions in my career was made just before I was diagnosed with breast cancer.

Like many other times in my life, I asked myself, "Should I do it? Why not?"

My plan was to study music at university and become a schoolteacher. It seemed like the perfect choice for me. I was well known as a pianist and accompanist and loved teaching kids as a Sunday school teacher and amateur figure skating coach. I had my life all planned out.

While I was in high school, a neighbour asked me to teach piano to her son. I had no plans to start teaching privately. Responding, "Why not," to her request changed my life forever and started my career as a piano teacher.

My plans changed due to complications following extensive knee surgery which required intense physiotherapy. While that surgery did not threaten my life, it certainly consumed months of it. I made the difficult decision not to return to university but to study piano privately, focus on my recovery, and continue teaching piano lessons.

Fortunately for me, I soon had a full schedule of loyal students. I should have been happy, but I wasn`t. I really felt that I could do better for my students, their parents, and myself. Something had to change. My ah-ha moment came to me one year when I had twelve beginner students. By the end of the week, I could not remember who I had said what to. There had to be a more effective way to provide quality lessons, honour the parents` financial investment, and use my time more efficiently.

Why not offer group piano classes? I had researched and knew that group lessons would be the solution. I invested in training, materials, and advertising as I launched myself into becoming a well-respected group piano teacher. Within three years of starting group classes, I outgrew my home studio, and I signed a lease to teach in a commercial space.

Group classes were working. My business was growing!

During this time, my right knee needed more attention. In the span of twenty-two months, I had three more knee surgeries, one of which saw me on crutches for four months. Amid the constant trips for physiotherapy and follow up appointments, I kept teaching, even though it meant dealing with considerable pain.

As I continued with my recovery, my studio continued to flourish. But I still wanted to give my piano students more. I felt they would really benefit from some occasional private lesson time. Why not offer a combination of group and private lessons?

I started drafting 'hybrid' piano lessons. Countless hours were spent researching materials, creating schedules, fee structures, and registration forms, as well as attendance records to track the group and private lessons. I was set to venture into a new lesson year using a new system, and new materials. I was excited.

It was at this time that Glory St. Germain invited me to become a member of the UMT team as Games Creator. I love creating - so, why not? My excitement grew.

However, that excitement was interrupted. On the last Friday of August, at my routine mammogram a lump was discovered, with the confirmation of breast cancer coming a week later. I was feeling completely overwhelmed, frightened, and lost. I started that first week of lessons in a complete fog. At the time, I did not know what the year held for me. The year brought many physical challenges. I had surgery and started back teaching six days later. I started chemotherapy part way through the lesson year, lost my hair, caught pneumonia which caused me to miss a month of lessons. After defering a few treatments I ended radiation a week after lessons finished for the year.

Still, with all of the challenges that year brought, my new hybrid system was a hit. Students and parents appreciated the hybrid lesson format as well as the condensed lesson year that came along with it.

I made it through that first year of hybrid lessons and went through cancer treatment at the same time. I was so relieved. I started into the next year of lessons but still had the nagging feeling that I could do more for my students. But why would I change anything? I had been through so much already!

I have never been completely satisfied with any method books that I have used. I would add or scratch out notes and skip pages altogether in an attempt to make the music work for my students. I was frustrated and no longer willing to just settle anymore.

I needed a solution. Why not create my own curriculum? As a composer and professional music games creator, I knew that I could create the materials I needed. I took my motivation, knowledge, and resources and got to work!

This time was so busy. I had numerous medical appointments. Nerve damage, accelerated arthritic degeneration, plus back and hand issues meant that I had many medical appointments and never ending physiotherapy. Still, I was not deterred from my quest to create the materials I needed.

My curriculum grew to include my original compositions, technique, as well as my own arrangements of classics and seasonal music. I included homework, attendance records, and numerous tips that I had created over the years. My material works for my students.

When I started my career, I had no thoughts of creating my hybrid piano lesson programme or writing my own curriculum, but I have done both. I had no idea that one of my job titles would be *Ultimate Music Theory Games Creator*, but it is.

I certainly did not foresee the physical challenges that would come my way, but they happened. Thankfully, each time I was able to answer, "Why not," when I wondered if I should keep going.

I now credit the challenging times in my life for inspiring me to be bold enough to answer, "Why not," with positive action and face risk head on. My challenges have come at great cost but have been worth it.

Answering, "Why not," has given me experiences and a sense of satisfaction that I could not have imagined.

I celebrate life everyday now as I live cancer free, waiting to see what the next 'why not' will bring my way.

Author Bio:

Joanne Barker, UMTC Elite Educator, Piano Teacher, Composer, UMT Creative Designer. Joanne has created a unique hybrid lesson system combining group piano with private instruction and written the lesson program used by her students.

https://UltimateMusicTheory.com

HELPING MUSIC TEACHERS TO SURVIVE AND THRIVE WITH ENTREPRENEURIAL SKILLS

Noreen Wenjen

United States

It was March 2020, and the dark shadow of Covid-19 was starting to rear its ugly head, spreading like wildfire and threatening our health, safety, and freedom. We no longer take this freedom for granted: the freedom to gather. Teaching online became an essential, required skill overnight for music teachers… and the entire world. Little did I know that one of the skills that I honed and tried to teach to other teachers at conferences for the past five years would be the key that would open doors for some music teachers and would lock out and 'lock down' everyone else. It became clear to me that this is the time for me to share my skills to help other teachers, as my mentors had helped me throughout my teaching career.

My journey as an independent music teacher began almost thirty years ago, and I have been teaching online for almost ten years. My love of music, technology, graphic design, and business has come together unexpectedly and helped to launch the second half of my teaching career as an entrepreneurial music teacher.

I have always had a love of technology and enjoyed working with computers. I learned basic programming skills in middle school and while working temp jobs and full-time with graphic design and marketing on Macintosh computers in the eighties. I worked for my sister's start-up company, MacTemps, the first Mac-based temporary agency, now called Aquent, a global Fortune 500 company. I learned many skills on the fly while working in the company or while out on a temp job. I designed newsletters and business proposals on Pagemaker/Indesign, managed corporate books using Quickbooks, built my communication skills, and discovered how a few motivated and creative people can build a small empire. Little did I know that this skillset, which is somewhat unique to musicians, was building my own unique footprint in the music world.

I went to college to study business, at least that was my original plan. Music always beckoned me. I performed in local and international competitions from age five until I went away to college at age seventeen, and I loved performing on the piano for live audiences. However, I did not think that a piano conservatory was the right place for me, as I had so many different interests. I wanted to stay close to home and only applied to a few California universities, as I had been a caregiver for my father, who had Parkinson's disease for many years. Unfortunately, my father passed the winter after college applications were turned in. In the spring, I chose the university with endless ocean views which allowed students to take classes from The University of California at Santa Barbara.

During college orientation, I learned that piano lessons for non-piano majors required out-of-pocket payments and was also notified that auditions were the following week. I switched my major to piano performance and auditioned the same week. Luckily, I had just performed a fifty-minute solo recital a few months earlier. I became a piano major, intending to switch my major at some point, and continued to take a breadth of classes including economics, French literature, impressionist art history, political science, and accounting, along with my piano major classes. These classes built my business foundation, and I continued to study and work in business, marketing, graphic design for the next six years.

When it comes to managing my music studios, an entrepreneurial switch inside my head flips on and lights up. Maybe it is because I love to see things grow. My Capricorn personality loves steadily working on things I am passionate about, sometimes obsessively. I have learned to be patient and not expect quick results. Do what you love to do and you will never work a day in your life. As teachers, we did not choose this career because we thought it was the easiest path for financial gain. We chose it because we could not live without it. Music is in our soul, and energy ignites when we share it with others. It is not enough to share this with passive listeners. We have the gift and love of teaching others.

Possibilities. Hope. Joy. Music. These are a few of the things that music teachers are made of. Every day, we instill these beautiful qualities back to our students. We help our students to lead creative, positive, well-rounded, and successful lives fueled by music.

I learned to reach outside the norms from my parents. My father was a math professor, a Fulbright scholar teaching real and abstract mathematics to students in which creativity and thinking outside the box was the goal. He spent a lifetime creating and solving proofs of what could be, working to solve something new that had no proven solution. My mother was possibly the most unfailing optimistic person that I've ever met, glass always full and spilling over with kindness and joy. Teachers are some of the most patient, optimistic individuals. We hope for the best for our students and believe in their growth and achievement. At some point, it is time to give back as a mentor, to help other teachers. For me, the time is now.

I created my course *The Entrepreneurial Crash Course for Music Teachers* to help other teachers not only survive but to thrive. I have been fortunate to have always had a two-year waitlist for my studios. Many teachers said that my book *Two-Year Waitlist: An Entrepreneurial Guide for Music Teachers* has helped them succeed. Music teachers want hands-on instruction to help them revamp their music studio and increase their income to pay their bills and not have to change career paths. I created my interactive online video course to walk teachers through each step and become an entrepreneurial small business owner. I have been able to help teachers double their student registrations and raise their income immediately. I am so happy to have helped teachers, especially during this challenging time.

Author Bio:

Noreen Wenjen is a nationally recognized piano teacher and author of *Two-Year Wait List: An Entrepreneurial Guide for Music Teachers, Entrepreneurial Crash Course for Music Teachers*, Past-President for CAPMT.org, MTNA SW-Div-Director-Elect and Torrance Business-Person of the Year.

https://wenjenpiano.teachable.com/

HOW TO BE A NATURAL MUSICIAN

Thulane Akinjide-Obonyo

Zimbabwe

Frustration is what I felt when I heard Fanyana say, "Play this after me." I was overwhelmed with just how much I did not know about music. There I was learning township jazz from a blind saxophone master, and I could not even hear what the first note was. I could not play by ear at all. I seriously believed that there were easier ways of learning music and this was not one of them. It took over two hours in order for me to learn two lines of a song, and all the while my saxophone teacher kept laughing at me, saying, "I thought you told me you knew how to play the saxophone."

This incident inspired me to find a simple way to teach saxophonists how to play by ear. Rappers really and truly do not have to learn how to sound out words; they speak the language; they must just learn how to rhyme with it. Birds don't have to learn how to sing; they are simply born singing the same tune. So, why is it, we seem to lose the ability to play what we hear? I say lose the ability, because, if you look at young children, they are all able to sing what they hear without hesitation, but us, older kids, seem to have lost that.

Self-doubt is the reason why. I remember the first time I was dropped from choir. I was thirteen years old and had been studying with the same piano teacher for the last six years. I had just started high school and really did not care about the choir audition. After all, I knew the choir master personally and she was my teacher. There was no way I would not make choir. After all, when I was six, I got the lead role in a production of *The Pied Piper of Hamelin.* I was really good at singing then. I knew I could sing; after all, I could sing then so why not now. My teacher told me I had no talent for singing and I would have to wait until my voice settled. To this day, I have no idea what that means. For all you, 'older kids,' it turns out the secret to playing by ear is singing.

After many attempts to fix the singing issue, I realised something. Singing is natural. I know that seems obvious to many but try and listen to the latest Taylor Swift song and play it straight away on your instrument. I bet you will struggle. Hearing and playing is not something many of us musicians are taught to do.

That is because aural awareness is not obvious to you, until you are asked that fateful question, by a well-meaning loved one, "Could you play me Bruno Mars's Uptown Funk?" and you freeze up like a deer blinded by headlights.

The desired outcome of that conversation is, "Sure, let me hop on the piano and play that for you."

Your answer may be, "Well, not right now, I would not like to spoil the party." Or any excuse that you can think of to get out of having to play by ear. It is the one skill that most musicians avoid. And yet the outcome you want is quite simple, to be able to hear and play any tune, automatically.

The major obstacle in being able to do this is the realisation that playing by ear is a learnable skill. I spent decades feeling sorry for myself thinking that playing by ear was something magical that only the extremely talented could do. What changed the game for me was the realisation that learning to play by ear had a method. And that method is mostly based on mass repetition, which is what most musicians, like me, are used to. Once that was realised, I knew that I could learn to play by ear as long as I could apply the method and rinse and repeat enough times to make it stick.

The method is simple, but there were other demons that I had to overcome in order to successfully learn to play the saxophone by ear.

Anger, crippling anger was one of them. This anger flowed from knowing that past teachers and other friends had lied to me. They had made the idea of playing by ear seem complicated. Playing by ear is simple - in many ways too simple. That is why the system of 'how to teach it' is overlooked.

There are also the naysayers who speak about the need to be a natural musician, whatever that means. That some people are born talented and gifted at music? Those wise teachers can see their talent at a young age and know that they were destined for greatness. The idea you are born with great musical ability and you don't acquire it through sweat and hard work was an obstacle.

The most difficult obstacle for me to overcome was the idea that if I could not play solos, pop songs, and children's songs instantly by ear, I was somewhat less talented than those who seemed to do it so effortlessly. I thought there was something wrong with me as I did not have what it took to be at that level of mastery.

The reality is that anyone can learn to play by ear, and the method to do so is extremely straightforward even though it requires a lot of repetition.

The myth that some are born talented while others are not is a major obstacle that I had to overcome to be successful. This caused me to delay learning to play by ear myself. Now, I have learned how to play by ear; I have created a program where I now teach others how to do so.

The talent myth is the most dangerous myth in music education – that some are born with perfect pitch and certain talents that allows them to be great musicians. Nothing could be further from the truth.

Musicians are made, not born.

Author Bio:

Thulane Akinjide-Obonyo, is a professional saxophonist and saxophone coach. He specialises in teaching people how to play the saxophone by ear so that they may unlock the true power of jazz and traditional folk music.

https://www.facebook.com/playsaxnow

BECAUSE OF A LITTLE GIRL FROM RWANDA; WHY I CREATED A COLOR CODED MUSIC PROGRAM

Sarah Lyngra

United States

More than twenty years ago I was living in Copenhagen, Denmark when I had my first student with severe learning difficulties. She was eight years old, from Rwanda, and had been adopted by a woman from Brooklyn, NY and her husband, a French speaking man from Ouagadougou. They had a nanny from Ghana, who spoke English and her local African dialect. The parents had been U.N. Aid workers in Rwanda during the genocide when they adopted her. At a very young age she had been exposed to atrocities there.

She was behind in school, particularly with language, fine motor control, and impulsivity. Her parents told me that they had no expectations that she would be able to learn much but were simply happy to find her a piano teacher.

She was a lovely girl, smiling and happy, and completely distracted by everything around her. Keeping her at the piano was a challenge when she was busy discovering all the nooks and crannies of our apartment.

From her first lesson, the concept of naming a piano key with letters was confusing. She was unable to describe notes on lines and spaces; they all looked the same to her. Directions such as left and right, and up and down were perplexing. It was worse for her when combining directions, notes on the page, and connecting them to keys on the piano.

Her fine motor skills weren't well developed; for the first months of lessons, she preferred to use only the pointer finger of her right hand for everything.

During a lesson a month or so in, I picked up some highlighter pens and, as an experiment, decided to color code the notes. If this worked, she would make progress, and if they didn't, we would try something else.

Highlighters were clunky, weird colors which bled through the page. I can't remember which colors we used, though I remember neon pink, yellowy green, purple, blue and a watery brown. Very quickly, my student picked up the concept that a colored note corresponded to a key on the piano. It didn't matter that she called the keys the colors, one pink, another brown. She was making the connection between notes on the page and music.

Her eyes started tracking better as well; she was training her eyes to move from left to right across a page of music. In the beginning, I pointed to each note, but over time, she was able to track from left to right on her own.

Her parents had told me that they weren't very good about sitting with her to practice. I think for them, keeping up with schoolwork was enough. At her first recital, I sat next to her at the piano, pointed to the notes, and guided her second finger to the correct keys. Four months later, at her second recital, she sat at the piano by herself, and was able to use all ten fingers and didn't need help tracking.

After the recital, with tears in their eyes, her parents told me how amazed they were. They had no idea that she had made so much progress.

Unfortunately, my husband and I moved a few months later and we lost touch. This was before social media. She's in her mid 30s now.

Connecting with students like her was the beginning of my journey to *Why I Created a Program* which uses colors for coding music, and why I create editions of music books that are accessible for all students. This student may have been the start of color-coding music, but why I continue is influenced by several other things.

When my son was in kindergarten and first grade, he wasn't thriving. He was tested for learning difficulties when he was seven. Before doing anything else, the psychologist who tested him advised us to have him checked out by a developmental optometrist. For the next ten years we learned a lot about how vision works as he spent hundreds of hours doing vision therapy. As a piano teacher, it was fascinating. One could say it was eye opening.

How music is read is based a lot on how music is seen. Students with poorly functioning eyes— not just being able to focus, but the ability to track notes across the page, and visually process those notes— are much more likely to memorize their music and more likely to be poor readers. Children and adults with learning difficulties often have complicated issues with how their eyes work.

My teaching studio has always been an experimental lab to try new ideas and test these ideas to see what works. Technology today has made it much easier to create colored scores of music with layouts that are based on how people actually see and read. Digital formats have made it possible to make the music available worldwide.

Using Sibelius (the music notation program), a music xml file, and email or a chat program, I create colored editions of what my students want to play in minutes. Sharing it in a lesson is easy with online technology. Twenty years ago, I did this with high-lighter pens which bled through. What a change.

I teach adults, students with special needs, and teens, and every day, I am reminded why I create colored editions. For some of my students, having visually accessible scores make the difference between playing a piece and never learning a piece.

Music is universally human. Creating scores that are easier for students to learn from and play brings more music and music makers into the world. That's why I do what I do.

Author Bio:

Sarah Lyngra, owner of *Yellow Cat Publishing*, is an online teacher, author, and blogger who teaches internationally. Her color-coded scores make her very popular with students who want to play more pieces brilliantly.

www.couchtoconcerthall.com

THE POWER OF ADDING FREE VALUE TO THE WORLD

Christopher Siu

Canada

As a pianist, composer, orchestrator, singer/songwriter, and YouTuber, my WHY never really came into focus until December of 2020. I had always been involved in music from a young age, but the tail end of 2020 really gave me time to sit down, reflect, and truly realize my WHY.

Let me explain.

When I was five years old, I began playing the piano. My parents told me I loved it, and that I progressed rather quickly, achieving my Levels nine and ten certifications at nine and ten years old respectively, and my ARCT diploma at age fourteen. However, although I enjoyed performing for others, I was never truly happy doing it. I didn't know why but something about performing other people's music was never completely satisfying.

It wasn't until I was in grade nine or ten when two friends of mine inspired my love for composing and producing music on the computer. Anton was a talented pianist and saxophonist who frequently composed short jazz pieces on the piano and watching him play every time made me smile and feel, 'I want to do that.'

Meanwhile, Ryan was an aspiring DJ who knew how to work all the knobs, controllers, and consoles, creating his own electronic music. I had the wonderful opportunity to give writing a go during music class when our teacher asked us to play around with GarageBand on the iMacs in the classroom. I must've written twenty short ideas that day, and shortly after, I'd written my first song with vocals: *Refreshed*. I was listening to bands like *Marianas Trench* during that time, so I drew influences from pop and punk music, in addition to my classical roots, and Disney songs to create my very first song.

Over the next few years, as I studied Classical Piano Performance in university, a friend of mine introduced me to Kontakt, a popular software used to play back sample libraries to create music with virtual instruments on your computer. It was then when I caught the bug for composition, creating my YouTube channel while I was in second year (2017), and sharing what I knew about writing, production, and arranging, on a weekly basis. I didn't know why, but I had a feeling that if I kept adding value to the world, people would begin to notice, and eventually it would pay off in some way.

At the same time, I began teaching piano as well to begin earning a regular income. It wasn't my favourite thing to do, but it allowed me freedom to work on what I enjoyed more (composing, doing freelance orchestration, and creating YouTube videos). My channel continued to grow for the next few years as I continued creating content, as well as growing my student base. However, I was overwhelmed as my schedule was increasingly tight as I took on more and more piano students.

And then, Covid-19 hit. All of the regular in-person lessons, frequent travel, and freelance jobs I had had, came to a halt. To be honest, I was relieved. I feared that I would never be able to free up my schedule to simply write the music I enjoyed writing the most. Although I enjoyed helping others by teaching, it never gave me complete satisfaction. In turn, it allowed me to double down on my YouTube channel. In fact, I committed to uploading one video per day in March of 2020, increasing my subscriber base exponentially. I also reached more people in my niche of composition, orchestration, and producing music on the computer. In addition, I began following a business coach on YouTube whose background was also in music, and he was making a living selling online courses. I then realised I wanted to give this monetization model a go.

If I could make a living helping others and sharing valuable information that could make a difference in people's lives, that's the perfect win-win situation.

So, in June and July of 2020, I created, filmed, and released my first ever full online course on orchestral music composition, entitled *Cinematic Music Creation*. Fortunately, I had a successful launch, which fueled the fire and gave me further incentive to continue down this path of freely providing value to others while earning an income.

The only issue was that the last piece of music I composed was for that particular course, and I hadn't written anything since July. November and December proved to be a turning point for me as I considered my why as I wasn't truly expressing myself creatively through my music. I then remembered that songwriting was my first love, because not only did I love to write music, but had been singing around the house my whole life, even when I annoyed my parents.

I bit down on the fear of lyric writing and simply committed to writing a new song, drawing on Covid and the political situation at the time for inspiration. The result was my song *Empty Holes*, which thankfully was very well received by my online audience.

This was when I discovered my true why.

The feedback I heard ranged from, "The melody, lyrics, and

orchestration really moved me," to "I actually had Covid myself and your song helped me get through the recovery period," and these comments gave me the spark and direction I needed.

Not only could I provide value to others by uploading weekly tutorials on creating music but people actually found my music relatable, meaningful, and emotional. That's all you can really ask for as a composer and songwriter. So, I committed to writing a ten-song album, fully completed, by my birthday in late August.

At the time of writing this (March 2021), I have five songs wrapped up, and am very much looking forward to seeing what emerges over the next few months. To add icing on the cake, two of my subscribers offered me their services free of charge: one offered to mix and master my album and the other wanted to create artwork for the album. This blew me away.

It truly demonstrates the value of creating a difference in someone else's life, and how it can come back to reward you if you stay the course, and continue helping people in what you love the most. So, all in all, that's my why.

Why do I do what I do? Because in writing music, creating regular content, and providing value to the world, I can get paid by selling online courses and memberships, and will be able support my future family. There's nothing better than that.

Author Bio:

Christopher Siu is a pianist, composer, singer/songwriter, YouTuber, and orchestral arranger with a degree in Classical Piano Performance from the University of Toronto. He works in virtual orchestration and in a variety of styles.

https://www.christophersiu.com/

IMITATE, ASSIMILATE, INNOVATE - IT'S LIKE MAGIC

Paul Myatt

Australia

As I heard the words, "You need to imitate, assimilate then innovate," it instantly struck me, this is exactly the process we train our *Forte School of Music* teachers to use. It's been working for over twenty-five years. Now we are teaching a whole new generation of piano teachers through our work in *The Studio and Piano Teaching Success* online TV show.

Learning requires us to start with the basics which is most naturally done through the process of imitation. Let's think about babies learning to speak or us learning to cook. Once the information is assimilated, or embodied, we can then begin to use it. And once we are confident and competent, we can then innovate in terms of music that's composing, improvising, arranging, or performing.

As Director of Education and co-founder of *Forte School of Music*, it's been a journey. We started out in 1994 by embracing the natural learning process of language - listen > sing > play > read > write - and applied it to teach the universal language of music. That worked well, but the game changer was when we started to move.

Being naturally kinesthetic myself, I've always known deeply that moving is integral to my own learning. I was the kid in the class with 'ants in his pants'. I'm not sure if this is an Australian expression or not but you get the idea. I couldn't bear being chained to a desk all day not able to move. I was the number one volunteer - I'd do anything to move.

I'm not alone. Many people are highly kinesthetic learners and what I know, and research has proven, is that everyone learns better when they move.

What frustrates and disappoints me is when I read the 19th century solutions put forth by teachers in Facebook groups for our 21st century students. I'm passionate about meeting children where they are at. When a child has difficulty in reading, we shouldn't be thinking of sacking them or writing him of her off. Difficulty or reluctance to read music could be for any number of reasons. It may be a problem with reading or that they have an awesome ear and playing by ear is just easier.

Reading without an auditory back up is like learning to speak another language without ever hearing it. They go hand in hand. And music after all is an auditory artform not a visual one.

Reading is a complicated skill and requires many things to come together to achieve mastery. Some read easily. Some don't. After over thirty years of teaching experience, I have found that just about every student learns to read in their teenage years, you've just got to get them there.

When I started out teaching piano, what I didn't know then, was we all learn best when we move. And when movement is combined with a killer aural development program, reading comes naturally over time and... the results, well they are astounding.

The success stories are wide and varied, and it amazes me

what kids can do. I know with all my heart that there is magic in teaching music. Here's a couple of stories from my brag book...

Tom came to me as a shy three-year-old who wasn't able to speak. His speech therapist had recommended music lessons as an alternative to ongoing speech therapy. That shy little boy recently achieved 98% for his grade eight Trinity College piano exam. I'm so proud of Tom. He is a musician's musician. He is able to play jazz and improvise at the drop of a hat as well as perform on stage as a classical pianist. He's even taught himself guitar, bass, drums, and how to multi-track record. Tom has played in two amateur Broadway musicals, regularly plays gigs in bands at clubs, and plays in Australian trumpet virtuoso James Morrison's student Jazz band. Tom is keen to pursue a musical career with plans to study at Sydney Conservatorium of Music. He typifies everything that I am so passionate about when teaching.

Bastien has gone down the pop singer/composer-performer route, writing, and performing his own songs. Bastien has performed in Carnegie Hall and stars in local musical productions in Singapore where he now lives. He's giving music a go for a year, and then it's on to medical school to become a doctor.

Alex was your everyday normal kid. Average in the class. Thank goodness he was in class where all the learning happens in the lesson, so even if they don't practice during the week, they tend to remember what has happened because it is embodied. Not much practice happened there for a while; however, everything fell into place when he became a teenager. All the things we'd been doing that weren't making sense to him, like the keyboard harmony, chords, and playing by ear, started to come together like a jigsaw in his brain, and he started to explore improvising and composing. Alex's goal now is to be a composer. He has a love of music from all periods and is now writing arrangements and compositions that mix styles and genres.

And a couple younger ones, Charlotte loves to sing in stage musicals and has performed with the Australian Opera. Cassidy is a singer-songwriter currently working on a song to present to a record label.

I am astounded at how varied each of these students' musical interests are and am humbled that the one thing they all have in common is me. Other things they have in common is that they have all learnt in group lessons at *Forte School of Music* using the *Whole Body Learning* approach. Most of them started music with me as little ones.

My ultimate goal is always to teach myself out of a job, to become the Piano Coach. This is when a student directs the learning using me, the teacher as a coach to achieve the goals they wish to achieve. All of these kids have been through the imitate, assimilate phases and are now innovating - it's where the magic really happens. Yeah, success and magic.

(* quote from Virtuoso Jazz Trumpeter Clark Terry.)

Author Bio:

Paul Myatt is co-founder of twenty-six-year-old *Forte Music School* network with over 7000 students in Australia, New Zealand and the UK and *Piano Teaching Success*. He is a passionate piano teacher, performer, author, composer, and workshop presenter.

https://pianoteachingsuccess.com

CONNECTIONS, VISIONS, AND DRIVE

Rebecca Featherstone

Canada

Throughout this project, I listen to my gut, and I don't let anything else get in the way.

In the last year, I've decided that, more often than not, listening to yourself is more important than following the advice of others. Arrogant? Maybe. But I believe in my dream, and it's worked so far.

There are always going to be times of major self-doubt in a big project like this. Am I doing the right thing? Have I made the right decision? Will the choices I make now affect the program down the road in a negative way? These are sometimes stressful emotions to go through, especially in the early stages of a startup.

Some days I want to pack it all in and go back to home-schooling my kids and baking bread and muffins to take on our nature hikes. But other days, I'm geared up and ready to rock.

I've learned over the years to not focus on the negative but rather find a way to a solution. It usually works out, and if it doesn't, then it's not the end of the world. I will still be here. My family will still be here. I am still breathing. Taking that risk is what makes it all worth it.

What is the point of life if you don't take risks?

As women, we have something profound inside us called intuition. Some of us are tuned in to it and some need a little help, but I assure you it's there. I read a really great book many years ago, but I can't remember the name. I remember it said to be on the lookout for the small clues life puts in front of you. For example, that same stranger you always see on the subway might have a message for you if you'd just stop and listen. This is how I started *Musicology*. The series of connections that brought me to this point is crazy, almost too weird to believe.

I am a typical Canadian piano teacher I suppose. I started playing piano when I was four. I'll never forget my first piano teacher, Angus Macleod. I think everyone remembers the teacher who changed their lives if they were lucky enough to have one. Angus was a funny old guy, completely dedicated to teaching. He would ride his bike in his tweed jacket and meet me at the local church to teach me. When I was applying to the Mohawk College music program years later, he'd drive up to Hamilton to help me prepare for my exams. I'll never forget his dedication to his students. He continues to inspire me.

I didn't always plan on teaching music as a career; I wanted to become a kindergarten teacher. After I graduated from university, I started teaching privately and found I was good at it, so I started hiring more teachers as everything started to grow. I cared deeply about all of my clients and the teachers and wanted the best for them. We had a great community feeling there.

Fast forward twenty years to the beginning of the global pandemic and I not only had a music school to run, but I was also the CEO for a major tech startup. Huh? How the heck did that happen? I'm going to let you in on a little secret – don't always assume that life will work out the way you planned.

I first got the idea for the *Musicology* app after a conversation with my accountant about what was lacking with the major video conferencing platforms out there. I saw the very clear need, from a first-hand perspective, for a video conferencing app built specifically for teaching music online with all the tools teachers needed. Not just any tools, but in fact, a completely interactive experience bringing the teachers and students together again. But who was going to build this vision?

My accountant, who I know through my high school piano teacher's son, introduced me to some amazing developers in Ottawa. The best part: they were hobby musicians with musical backgrounds and a *huge* passion for gaming. It was a perfect match. Throughout this entire project, they've consistently exceeded my expectations.

From there, it was all about connections. Connections are what really drives a project like this. Getting the right people for the team. One important factor for me is that everyone working on this project was a Canadian with some musical experience. My leadership coach is an amazing guitarist. He then referred me to a top advertising executive in Toronto who has a passion for the banjo. Even the government funded organizations that are providing us with professional support either play a musical instrument or have kids of their own that are learning. Their eyes get so big when I pitch our app to them—they always seem completely astounded and immediately tell me they want to be involved. It never fails.

Having people by your side who support you and want the best for you is a great feeling and one that I hope to give it all back one day. It's an emotional rollercoaster, but totally worth it. A few things that have helped me stay calm during this transition in my life is to have routine, a balanced diet, a long, daily walk, and yoga once a week. These things have kept me sane, and I believe they will continue to keep me sane throughout the whirlwind of what is expected to come in the next year.

I'm a music teacher, that's how I know how well *Musicology* works. I can't wait to see the smiles on teachers' and students' faces when they connect on *Musicology* and see how smoothly it functions and how it addresses their unique needs. Why? Because this is an app created for music teachers, by music teachers, and our plan is nothing short of revolutionizing the way music is taught online in Canada and around the world.

Author Bio:

Rebecca Featherstone is a graduate of McMaster University and has been teaching piano for over 20 years. She owns a multi-teacher studio in Toronto and is the CEO of *Musicology*; a video conferencing platform with built-in interactive tools for teaching.

https://www.musicology.ca

Natalie Eastman

United States

I started creating vocal-development courses and programs in my music studio for a host of reasons - why?

1. To show my students their progression of growth in vocal development through the use of benchmarks, the structure of courses, and programs provided.
2. To gather and logically synergize pedagogical influences from several different vocal genres (Bel Canto/classical/opera, contemporary/pop/rock/folk, and musical theatre/Broadway, primarily). Just like I do when I'm working with my voice students, I wanted to integrate the best, most helpful elements, and exercises from various singing methods and schools of thought and practice.
3. To create dependable income by automating as much

of the pedagogical process as I could. Courses can be used and sold in and of themselves, independent from private lessons. Also, they can be broken up, rearranged, and/or rejoined with sections/units from other courses or programs.

4. To automate as much as I could of the foundational, repetitive portions of singing instruction, to allow students to self-pace.

5. So, students could use those program structures to self-direct and self-pace, and I could focus more on coaching. As a result of the front-loading students do using the coursework, in our private lesson we can fine-tune, customize, and apply exercises, and knowledge to their performance-singing.

6. To establish visually to site visitors that I have a system; testimonials help them see that the system works. Systems add credibility to your studio and coaching.

Any of those would be excellent reasons for you to start creating programs and courses, too. But more than all of those good reasons, I found over time the reason that is most important and valuable to me:

Creating the program structures helped me think.

Those structures, I observed, kept my students and me on track and from wandering around in both life and vocal development, always starting but never finishing. Students and I can both see the flow. We each can track progress. We can also see endpoints, which help us see light at the end of various voice-development tunnels.

Let me explain why this is so important to me.

Thirty years ago, an executive consultant for The Highlands Group told me that I had something called "High Idea Productivity."

"Natalie," she said, "the good news is that you are both intelligent and highly capable in many areas. You've scored high in areas of multiple intelligences and you are a little bit 'off the charts' when it comes to the various kinds of skills we tested. That's the good news. The challenge you're going to face, though, is finding a career path that's going to keep you challenged and attentive to what you're doing."

I recall thinking at that time, "Well, that kind of sounds like I'm pretty smart... but is this good or bad?"

Defining myself or my abilities by categories assigned to me by tests and profiles has never interested me, although I do find them interesting. The danger, I believe, is living into the diagnosis you've received like it's an identity, rather than a possibility. That can potentially lead to unhelpful emotional and mental postures such as fearfulness about trying something new. This could be challenging or self-limiting based on the diagnosis.

That said, skills inventories can also guide you helpfully toward better interactions with your abilities and with the people with whom you work and live. Their goal, usually, is to allow you an understanding of yourself that helps you walk in your strengths, rather than your weaknesses.

It behooves all of us to look for opportunities that play to our strengths and minimize our weaknesses. Do what you're good at, rather than what's a struggle, and allow others to do the activities that they're good at or utilize tools that achieve the same effect.

The issues my skills inventory and the suggested description/diagnosis of High Idea Productivity helped expose, though, were (1) the challenges I could potentially face, and did face, of containing my idea production; (2) the challenges I could face sticking with an idea or group of ideas I'd produced; and (3) the ultimate fact that I was, as an adult, going to be identified as a clear case of undiagnosed ADD.

Thirty years ago, when I was tested, the term Attention Deficit Disorder existed, but was generally known only to those impacted by a relevant situation.

Little did we know that ADD would ultimately describe my brain's activity patterns. As an avid reader and fairly high-performing student, it wasn't on my radar. Yet, distraction and difficulty focusing characterized nearly every day of my life and every effort I expended. That effort could be reading one page of a book top to bottom, in order; or getting online for a quick second just' to check my email; completing a project on time; or self-organizing so I could find my keys, glasses, phone, or purse. Again.

Despite earning a master's degree, a doctorate, and publishing a significant academic-style volume, I have struggled to maintain focus throughout every endeavor that didn't have an impending deadline looming over my head. In fact, I learned to use deadlines, whether externally or internally imposed, to help me finish things. And I think that's partly what helped me turn to structured course creation.

As my music studio developed, I helped an increasing number of singers sharpen their skills and sing better and helped those who consider themselves non-singers or tone-deaf to sing. Over time, it began to dawn on me that (1) a lot of what I do with students I repeat, repeatedly; and (2) keeping track of their progress could be systematized. It took what feels like an embarrassingly long time to figure out how to develop processes I was using into a curriculum; but eventually I did, and it helps both my students and me. I enjoy the fact that by providing structure for imparting my unique pedagogical approach, I can help people with minds like mine that struggle with focus. I can also help them blossom and shine right alongside people whose brains, gratefully, function just fine.

I now find creating course structure helps me see the bigger picture. Additionally, having coursework created and running on autopilot inside my programs allows me the freedom to do what I do best: think, be in the moment with my student-clients, and produce more ideas to help and coach them to greater heights.

Do you dream of impacting others using your singing voice?

I can help you shorten the path & accelerate progress toward your best singing voice & greater performance confidence! Take my FREE 3-day Vocal Foundation Training course!

Author Bio:

Dr. Natalie Eastman is the owner and principal educator at *A Higher Note LLC*. She teaches voice, guitar, and piano, and beginner bass guitar. Her singing client list includes two Miss America contestants.

https://ahighernote.com/

FINDING MYSELF THROUGH ART SONG LAB

Michael Park

Canada

Art Song Lab (ASL) is a collaborative institute facilitating creative interaction between writers, composers, and performers from around the world to advance the genre of contemporary art song. Offering a 6-month collaborative opportunity which culminates in a week-long intensive program.

I've written that blurb so many times over the past decade, it's hard to distinguish my own experiences from those of the program. *Art Song Lab* has always been a profoundly collaborative effort so I can't take credit for all the work, but I also can't speak on behalf of anyone else. I express my deepest gratitude to my co-founders and all the participants and guest artists that I have had the honour of working with over the years, but here I want to focus on how I've grown from an opportunistic self-interested composer into a person who thrives on helping other artists make connections and create new work.

Back in 2009, I was a young composer eager to break into Vancouver's new music scene. I had a knack for writing vocal music, so naturally my social circle was full of singers and pianists. In that world, there's a real sense of 'learning from the masters', with a heavy emphasis on old dead guys. On vocal recitals, 'new music' often includes anything from the twentieth century, and it could be like pulling teeth getting them to program works by a living composer. Knowing that Vancouver was home to an internationally renowned art-song training program for singers and pianists, I teamed up with an enterprising poet and we pitched them an innovative idea: instead of having dozens of pairs focusing on Schubert and Goethe, we would write a new song that all the student pairs could study and perform. Of course, they politely declined... but something about our pitch resonated, and it was the faculty of that program that took the bait.

In 2010, I was thrilled to organize and participate in a workshop that focused on art songs by living composers and writers. It was surprisingly difficult to find those kinds of local collaborations, but this was a great opportunity to feature the song I'd written specifically for the workshop. Even before the event, it had turned out better than I could have hoped - not just students, but some of Canada's finest musicians were going to perform my music. On the day, the performances were stellar. No doubt I was on cloud nine, but there was another feeling in the air. It was so humbling to realize that everyone present: the singer, pianist, composer, poet, and the audience were all experiencing something that was so vital, and yet so rare. I mean having the creators and performers all together in the same room just having a conversation. At first the performers were focused on asking about notation and the composers' intentions, but when I deferred some of those questions to the poet I had worked with, it gave the performers permission to ask the poet directly. And for a world where singers spend so much time analyzing text on a page, this was nothing short of revolutionary.

In that room, there was a sense that the power of art song transcended the practices we'd been used to, and this was an experience we needed to share with the world.

In the early years of *Art Song Lab*, I towed the line between organizer and participant. We were constantly challenging the definition of 'Art Song' and pushing the artistic practice forward. I felt that all my organizing work was worth it for the opportunity to be part of such a vibrant community of artists. Through the benefit of hindsight, I can see that just creating and sustaining the program was the most important work I could be doing, but what drove me was my own compositional practice.

By about the third year, we had most of the kinks worked out and things were running smoothly. Having been a participant in the program twice, I stepped out of the spotlight and put my efforts into facilitating the experience for others. I wish I could say that I didn't feel like I was missing out, but my own sense of worth was still tied up in the individual pieces I wrote. I had seen dozens of composers and poets come through the program from all across Canada and the United States. Seeing them winning prizes and establishing their careers, I felt a strange mix of pride and jealousy. Since I wasn't winning competitions or grants, I felt like I was falling behind my peers.

One winter vacation, I was catching up with a friend in Toronto at a popular post-concert watering hole. He introduced me to some musician colleagues and the conversations flowed, along with the drinks. When our talks turned to our mutual love of art song, I told them all about having written the world's first interactive art song (sung ad-lib where the audience filled in the blanks), but was hesitant to mention my administrative work. As it turns out, I didn't even need to. Moments later, this Toronto singer I'd just met started telling me about a great new summer program for composers out west called *Art Song Lab*. He had just pitched me my own program!

I often think back to this moment as a turning point for me. Not only was it a great story to share with my colleagues back home, but it gave me insight into the kind of influence I could have. I had set out to make a name for myself in Vancouver, and here I was hearing that the little program I'd help create had a national reputation. At that initial workshop, my creative work helped to identify a powerful type of collaboration and connection that was lacking in the world of art song. I've created and continue to create songs that exemplify the important relationship between creators and performers, but it's not my music alone that will make the change we need. And so, I've embraced the behind-the-scenes work and take pride in knowing that the creative and administrative worlds are neither as separate nor codependent as I thought. It wasn't a sudden shift; I still struggled with feeling like I wasn't really an artist, but I started to truly see the value in what I was doing beyond simply being a means to an end. Why? Because I felt a sense of accomplishment and people were starting to take notice.

Author Bio:

Michael Park is a composer and pianist with a keen interest in speech, humour, and collaboration. His music aims to give audiences an experience beyond the realm of traditional concert-going.

https://www.michaelpark.ca

A BETTER WAY

Gillian Erskine

Australia

Almost from the beginning, after I got over an extreme bout of imposter syndrome, I thought, "Aaagh, there must be a better way."

A better way to learn music,

a better way to keep my students inspired and interested,

a better way to pass on this skill, this art form, this pleasure to others.

You see, I 'survived' music education rather than being inspired by it.

I was absolutely terrified of my first piano teacher and came very close to quitting after about a year or so. It was a miracle that I survived, and as a seventeen-year-old rookie piano teacher, I was determined to find a better way for my students. I was fairly ambitious for them though and didn't want to compromise on progress or achievement and yet I wanted them to find joy in learning and make this most pleasurable of pastimes, fun.

And so, the search began, a search for

the newest and best tutors on the market,

the best teaching techniques and methods,

the best resources and a way for me to make this into a real career.

Surely something was out there just waiting for me to discover.

I did the obvious things; I went to all the music warehouses searching for the latest and greatest courses. I studied with a teacher who specialized in diplomas and completed my ATCL & LCTL teacher's diploma. I was looking, and while there were some answers in there, I was yet to find my magic path.

I had started to fall in love with this profession, and yet, I had also begun to realize that my income potential was limited if I continued teaching private students. The ten weeks of school holidays were appealing, so the question became how do I make this into a real job with a real income that I could build a real life on?

I had already managed a dealer music school full of private students and could see that wasn't a financially viable model. Group teaching appeared to be a likely solution, but I didn't know how to provide a high-value lesson of which I could be proud. I didn't even know if it was even possible.

Then, I was introduced to a music education program that specialized in group teaching for young children, which I loved from the outset. I learned how to teach group classes and went on to own my own music school based on this system and become a trainer and instructor. After a few years, when an opportunity came to develop my own system with fellow music school owner, Paul Myatt, I stepped straight in.

Together, we launched *Forte School of Music* in 1994, and over the next twenty-six plus years, we've expanded in a small way throughout the world with seventeen amazing business partners at the helm of their own *Forte Schools*. Today, we are spread from England and Wales to New Zealand and across five states of Australia teaching around 7,000 students each week that learning music is fun.

When we work in our genius zone the time zooms by; there are never enough hours in the day and yet we don't even notice it. In the first few years, we were in a publishing frenzy working eighteen-to-twenty-hour days. We both had large music schools with some 1400 students between us who needed material and needed it immediately. We discovered that, rather than necessity, sheer need and drive can be the mother of all invention.

Our greatest challenge was figuring out how to transform our young, inexperienced, mostly university student teachers into extraordinary class teachers. We needed to do this super quick before they mowed through their respective students leaving our reputation and bottom line in shambles.

So, we started a project to develop a training system and resources center for our Forte teachers that continues today. We struck it lucky. Video cameras and technology started to become affordable, so we began to create a library of recordings of how to teach. Despite these being complete with the hairdos and fashionistas of the nineties, many of them are still in use today.

One of the best things we've done over the years is to be early adopters and creative thinkers around using technology in our business. We've seen the move from cassette tapes to CDs to a smartphone app, which drives us mad with having to invest in continual system updates, and lately to an online system for *Practice Buddy* – a practice companion. Sometimes, you just need to roll with the punches, do your best, keep going, and when all else fails get creative.

As musicians, we are creative beings, and being in such a small industry it is rare to have purpose-built software at our fingertips. Sometimes, it's just about looking at what we want to achieve and finding innovative ways to do it. The tech revolution hit quickly and yet it provided us with such a great opportunity to develop *Forte Practice Buddy* which is so much better than the cassette tapes we started out with originally.

Sure, it's been daunting at times. I can't think back to a time where I didn't need to constantly learn, learn, learn. Even recently, when feeling overwhelmed at a bunch of new tech systems I needed to understand, I wondered, "Could they just plug a microchip in so I can know all this stuff now?" Rest assured that you are not alone and it's just a matter of eating the elephant - one small bite at a time.

More than anything, know deep in your heart that you too have your own unique magic to bring to the world. Dream big, expand your thinking, become a lifelong learner and you too can build a program or a career of which you are proud.

Author Bio:

Gillian Erskine is the co-founder and CEO of *Forte School of Music and Piano Teaching Success* and dedicated to helping teachers around the world engage, motivate and accelerate success through whole-body learning and making music fun.

https://www.fortemusic.com/

MY MUSIC IS THE REASON I LIVE, LOVE, EDUCATE, AND INSPIRE

Edy Rapika Panjaitan

Asahan, North Sumatera, Indonesia

One of the numerous memorable moments that remain within me is being an orphan. I almost lost hope. My home is a small village which was never really on any map. My study of the piano early on in my life was near impossible. How can people from low economic backgrounds possibly have any way of learning an instrument? Piano has historically been played by people of high social status and not people like me, but I had big dreams.

Everyone has their own talent. For a short time, I enrolled on a piano course in a small town, which was far from where I lived. As I entered the building, I caught sight of a little boy, Jeremy, and I heard him playing *Beethoven's Sonata*. He must have been no more than eight years old. His playing was breathtaking, speechless. His playing moved me by its beauty. Shortly after I heard him, I decided I simply had to learn piano.

This was the beginning of my musical journey.

In the first three months my teacher confirmed that I had potential, even though I started at such a late date. At this point in time, believe it or not, I was seventeen years old. It was hard to contain this passion without feeling limited in what I could do. Most people give up at this stage because the mature mind tends to tell us that late starters are non-starters.

I can wholeheartedly say - It is never too late to start lessons on a musical instrument, no matter what your age might be. In my own experience, I have taught adults, even old-aged-pensioners, and they feel music is a fundamental part of their lives. Indeed, it helps their minds to remain strong in the face of aging. We should learn when the time is right for us, regardless of age, there are so many positive things that can emerge as a result of studying the piano.

I was struck with sudden revulsion that being a teacher of music was truly the most horrendous idea in my head. In hindsight, my long journey supported me and informed my final decision to become a promising music teacher.

The journey had begun, but I did wonder why I should not pursue a career in another field. What could I possibly benefit from with a future in music?

As I went along this fateful path, I had to accept my decision, and this is where my passion is to make itself known once again. During this education degree, I came to the realisation that teachers are gifted, dedicated, and passionate. Despite my introverted tendencies, I pushed myself to enter some piano competitions. I was taken aback when I won an award in a national competition. I remember the event so clearly, waiting in the queue until late evening in order to get a chance to practice. For me, perseverance was the key to my success.

Without discipline, I couldn't possibly have got what I wanted. Eventually, I completed my bachelor's degree and was given an award as the best undergraduate, graduating with predicate 'summa cum laude'. It was such an honour and a privilege. How ironic when compared with a time when I thought I would never teach.

I decided to do masters' degree study abroad. I was awarded

a full scholarship to study in Chengdu with world renowned piano experts. My dreams had finally come true. This was because I always give to the fullest of my ability. Eventually, I was able to graduate, though unfortunately, I could not celebrate this in China. I received a lot of guidance from many precious people. During this time, I won several prestigious prizes and awards in China. It was always a dream, and I had realised it. I now knew dreams will come true if you truly fight for them

In another journey, the German Consul in Chengdu invited me to present a residence concert before his very special guests representing eleven countries including the Consul General, notable businessmen, music professors, journalists, and artists. I was starstruck. At this point I was bursting with pride that I, originating from a tiny village, was able to achieve all of this.

During the recent pandemic, many people encountered a lot of stress, lost hope, and were not as productive as normally they might be. I was also ready to give in during my final semester because I was frustrated with online lessons, but I was able to overcome this. I told myself that I had to survive.

For the longest time I had toyed with the idea of establishing my own music school, and during this, I was able to put a plan into action. This was not because I needed a job, but rather, I felt I had to achieve something else and accomplish my mission to open a music school. From this came *Panda Piano Course*. The Panda idea itself came when I successfully achieved my dreams in the city of the Giant Panda, Chengdu.

This was going to be my mission: to educate and inspire students until they achieved their own success in music. I wanted to provide the best online piano lessons and masterclasses with international experts. As a result, we started to engage students from all over the globe. My aim was for every student around the world who desired to pursue their goals and needs in music would be able to do so at affordable prices. I am grateful that I have experts who come from all corners of the globe.

Our quote is "Abundant in Harmony". The black and white keys of the piano represent the colours of the Panda, and I hope we will create millions of beautiful melodies in perfect harmony. I want to share everything that I have; I return the good deeds that others have done for me. People inspire me when supporting, helping, loving and caring for each other.

I hope the journey will never end.

More recently, I won a composition competition composing a march for Indonesian overseas students in Alliance. I never imagined that I would become a composer. I believe the reason why I have to write music is truly inspired by Beethoven. He is my greatest inspiration.

I really hope that I can contribute more to composition, and everyone, one day, will hear this music. Never ever stop learning, fight for your dreams, as it is this that ultimately makes us who we are and why we influence those around us.

Author Bio:

Edy Rapika Panjaitan is the Founder and CEO of *Panda Piano Course* - high quality online piano lessons, and guidance masterclasses with international experts. Edy is a music educator, lecturer, pianist, arranger and composer.

https://pandapianocourse.com

MY MUSICAL JOURNEY: NOW AND THEN

M Ruth McCants

United States

Following the Dream

Once upon a time, a very long while ago (mid-eighties - twentieth century), I encountered a sound I had never heard. Standing in the town square in St.Thomas, Virgin Islands, the magical sound of a steel drum, better known as steelpan in the Caribbean islands, transported my inner child into an altered state of awareness. A lone teen girl stood pensively playing her magical instrument. Perhaps she was rehearsing for a performance. Or maybe, playing for an audience of one?

Finding the Path

My story of journeying toward my musical self is odd, ordinary, and unique. In fact, I believe becoming a musician is really about activating and releasing something that is within every person. As a seven-year-old, I didn't know my creative potential and abilities were evolving. Music was becoming a medium of expression for my life path. My early childhood play involved tracing music notes from old pieces of found sheet music and making sounds on an old upright piano that probably came out of the 19th century.

Here's a tiny bit of the backstory. In the 1950's, I lived in a house that was probably vintage 19th century, as a best guess. It was the kind of house where sections of it had to be closed off in the mid-western winters. Now, the most wonderful thing about this house was the piano that sat in a corner of the stairwell. Unfortunately, this was the part of the house that was unheated in the winter. You're probably wondering, 'a piano up against the stairwell'? Where did it come from? Who knows? Here is what my seven-year-old self-understood. I adored those foghorn sounds while watching most of the keys go up and down. There were a few permanently stuck ones. Yes, I would play in the winter, wearing my thick coat, gloves, and a hat.

At seven, my long, long journey and musical love affair began in earnest. The second-grade teacher in the tiny three-room school that I attended from kindergarten through third grade would become my first music teacher. My lessons began with an agreement between my mother and the teacher. In exchange for housekeeping work, I would have the opportunity to study piano. The first Saturday that I walked into my teacher's home and saw her grand piano I was in awe. I recall having a complete out of body experience as I touched those smooth keys and listened to that piano sing its song. Not to worry though, I still loved my beloved old foghorn piano because it was my best friend.

Over the course of a few months, I would leap into note reading with absolute delight and zeal. Another fabulous fun experience which occurred around the same time I was listening to my older cousins who lived across the street. All day long for months on end, I was treated to their playing of popular boogie woogie tunes of the day. On my foghorn piano, I attempted to play what I was hearing. I was not allowed to cross the street alone. So, I had to use my ear to connect with my cousins' music. Even now, boogie woogie and blues piano are still some of my favorite genres of music.

When I was eight, my family moved, but the beloved old foghorn piano would not be coming along. It would take years for me to realize that it was, indeed, my childhood security blanket (BFF), and I sorely missed it when it was left behind. From the ages of eight until I was sixteen, I kept hoping each year that I would come home one day and find a new piano.

When I turned sixteen, the mother of the cousins who had played the boogie woogie all those years before agreed to sell me that very rockin' boogie piano. Her words to me, "You can buy it for the number of years that you are old." I gladly gave her my sixteen dollars from summer work. Finally getting it home, I would still have an uphill climb. It would be difficult in a crowded house, finding practice time, and not having money for a teacher. The years would pass, and my musical journey would be a hit and miss situation.

Finally, as a twenty-seven-year-old grad student in education and psychology, and moving into my first apartment, I would rent a real piano, and look for my second music teacher. What I discovered during this time was that I possessed both tremendous amount of musical hunger and self-doubt in equal measure. I wanted to play everything but would have to start from scratch to even play the most elementary music.

Turning the Key and Opening the Door

The music program that I offer has developed from my long arduous journey that required tenacity, emotional fortitude, creative imagination, and staying true to my childhood dream. Even though I earned an advanced graduate degree and had a respectable career in academia for years, there was still something missing.

Countless years and many musical ups and downs later, I would come to understand just how important the inner child is to understanding the innate musicality that is within every person. My inner child musical self would not settle down until I applied, received acceptance, and earned a music school degree.

Nowadays, as a musician, teacher, and music business owner, I teach from the perspective that music is something released from the depth of creative possibilities and soul expression. I recall a student who studied piano with me for a couple of years. One day she said, "Piano is okay, but do you think I can study flute?" I congratulated her on following her insight and watched worried eyes sparkle with light as she moved toward her destiny.

With each student I encounter my desire and intention is to help them understand that music comes from within the individual. I definitely guide them through establishing the musical language, technique and foundational basics. Exploration of performance, composition, improvisation, while being open to creative possibilities is the price of admission to releasing the joy of playing.

Perhaps you are wondering if I ever became a steelpan player? A definite yes. A rare opportunity to play in a steel drum band came my way. My 'pan' is one of my most cherished instruments along with my piano, violin, and collection of frame drums. My musical journey continues.

Author Bio:

M. Ruth McCants, PhD, UMTC Elite Educator, teaches piano, theory, composition, and improvisation. Ruth offers an experiential connection with music in the form of sound vibration. She facilitates group drumming, toning, and the healing modality of Tapping (Emotional Freedom Technique EFT).

http://www.pianofunplayer.com

WHY I DIDN'T UNDERSTAND AND WHY I DO NOW

Glory St. Germain

Canada

You may wonder why a shy sixteen-year-old girl that didn't do well in her own piano lessons, barely passing her level eight piano exam and with no confidence in her musicianship skills would venture into the world and tackle all obstacles to become a piano teacher.

Why? The answer is simple: I wanted the money to buy a car. But what I discovered was the magic of music and the five teaching techniques that changed my life forever.

I remember teaching my dolls how to sing. Lining up the tall dolls to stand at the back, the pretty dolls with fancy dresses in the middle, and the floppy dolls who were never interested in the music lesson I was trying to teach lying on the side. Little did I know that someday this would turn into my life's work - teaching students of all learning styles and abilities the joy of music.

Things may seem smooth and easy for me now, but they weren't always this way. I grew up in a musical family, and music lessons were like brushing your teeth, you did it every day. The trouble was it didn't come easily to me. My father taught me the importance of learning music theory as it was part of my studies, but honestly, I just didn't get it.

My teacher did not really explain any of the theory concepts; it was here's a book, memorize the terms. So, I was confused. Why did chords have different names? Why did a **V** chord go to a **I** chord? Why did a major key have a relative minor key? Why were there letter names at the top of the staff on something called a lead sheet?

I didn't know why. And that's why I was not a confident music theory teacher.

Despite spending years trying to figure out exactly how to teach music theory effectively, and spending thousands of dollars on books and training, I couldn't find effective teaching materials.

The truth is, I had a successful piano teaching studio, but my self-confidence as a theory teacher was not happening. I have always been someone who would set goals and achieve them, even if that meant I only got a mark of 60% on theory exams - hey I still achieved a pass, right?

I almost gave up.

I remember the day I was sitting at the piano, feeling overwhelmed about how my own learning in music theory had been such a frustrating experience for me. You know when you just hit the wall and wonder if you can ever turn things around?

Then, my student skipped in the door with this big happy grin, eager to learn and positive that I was an amazing teacher. I thought, if my student can have so much confidence in me, I should have confidence in myself.

Something in me just snapped.

The years of self-shame, imposter syndrome, and feeling not

good enough, not smart enough, or even talented enough, that I've felt all my life, started to explode within me.

In that instance, I knew it was time for a change.

That was when I realized how I felt about myself and the way that I was taught. I knew the way I was teaching was my responsibility. I didn't have to put up with feeling this way anymore.

My life changed that day - not the music notes on the page, but the determination in me to do something differently about my teaching techniques so my students wouldn't have to go through the same frustrations that I did.

I went on a massive search, reading and researching how to write books for effective learning and discovering innovative techniques that allow students to reinforce and recall incredible amounts of knowledge with amazing accuracy.

I created fun drills that dramatically increase retention and comprehension.

Studying music theory can be a drag. As educators, we know music theory is a necessary component of development, but how can we engage students with enthusiasm?

I read a ton of books; I even tried telling jokes - lol, whatever it takes, right?

To be honest, I was a little discouraged and losing hope that things would ever change for me.

The negative self-talk came rushing in. I thought to myself, "Maybe I am destined to be a boring teacher. Maybe I don't deserve to have a successful teaching business."

After a while, I realized that if I couldn't find a program that worked for me, it was time for me to write a program that worked.

The aha moment - my life changed dramatically when I discovered the magic in five teaching techniques to engage my students in a system to learn theory faster in different ways.

That's when something life-changing happened.

Every day, I would dedicate my focused attention to writing

the *Ultimate Music Theory Workbook Program*. The biggest challenge was researching and getting started with the very first publication.

I thought all would be solved once I started writing, but I soon discovered that there was much more to unfold.

I needed to embrace advanced training, implement systems, and understand how students learn differently in order to write the *UMT Program* effectively.

I stuck to my plan and each time I faced a challenge, I saw it as an opportunity to learn something new. I could hear my mother's voice shouting, "It's not overwhelming - it's an opportunity."

I don't know which was more exciting - when I sold my first book or when my first student scored 100% on her theory exam using the *Ultimate Music Theory Workbook Program*.

As time passed, my self-confidence grew as did the *Ultimate Music Theory Program*.

And that's when I discovered why the five proven teaching techniques had helped me achieve success in writing the UMT Program which now includes over fifty theory workbooks and online teacher training programs around the world.

I created the UMT dream team.

We've helped thousands of learners literally double their speed of music theory skills advancement. We are committed to creating great study tools to accompany all *UMT Workbooks* and to continuing to advance the effectiveness of our learning technology.

That kickstarted an amazing transformational journey in my life as I continued to develop new ways of making learning music theory easier.

I want to share this gift with you.

Go to UltimateMusicTheory.com to get your free *Ultimate Music Theory Teachers Guide* - so you can discover the five proven teaching techniques and implement them into your teaching and discover your Why.

Author Bio:

Glory St. Germain is an International Bestselling Author of 50+ *Ultimate Music Theory Books, The Power of WHY Series,* and host of *Global Music Summits.* Glory is the creator of the *UMT Certification Course, UMTC Elite Educator Program,* and *UMT Teachers Membership Expert Business Coach.*

https://UltimateMusicTheory.com

AFTERWORD - THE MAGIC OF MUSICAL RELATIONSHIPS

Glory St. Germain

One of the most powerful relationships we have is our relationship with music. And for all of you music-savvy people out there, you may think I'm referring to the musical relationships themselves, as in major keys and their relative minor keys, or dominant chords and their relationship to the tonic, but I am talking about the real meaning of our relationship to the music itself.

My musical relationship has been like any other relationship one might have: one of love, disappointment, frustration, uplifting, motivating, reflecting, in sickness and in health for better or for worse. My relationship with music has shaped my life in a profound and extraordinary way. Born on Christmas Day to the resounding sound of musical celebrations put me on my path to becoming a musician. Through frustrating hours of practice, sometimes disliking the experience and despite the immense discipline required through perseverance, I became a piano teacher at the age of sweet sixteen. I was young and naïve, not realizing that I didn't really know anything about teaching at that time. Now as a professional educator, I realize in retrospect,

I should give them all their money back. But the truth is, I gave all those students — those musicians - a start in their own relationship with music.

You might recognize the global symbol of the Treble Clef — what does this represent to you? What do you think about or feel inside when you see the symbol of the Treble Clef? This symbol — the Treble Clef, also known as the G Clef, is one of the most powerful symbols in the universe. Why? Not because the G Clef stands for Glory St. Germain (that's what I actually told my students, you know the ones I taught at age sixteen), but this universal symbol of the Treble Clef represents the relationship of music - that can change the fabric of your life.

As an educator, I have seen many students struggling with relationships — with their parents, their friends, their siblings, and themselves. Often frustrated, depressed, afraid, and even suicidal — turning to music — to the one relationship they could count on — to pour their heart out and play their music as an escape. Many people, including the great Billy Joel, who attempted suicide when despondent over his failing career, later wrote one of his greatest hits *You're Only Human* dealing with teenage depression and suicide. For a musician, their instrument is often their most treasured possession. They often take better care of their instrument than they do themselves. Tormented between the music and drug addiction - the late jazz guitar genius Lenny Breau would often sleep with his guitar. It is a little more difficult as a pianist to sleep with your instrument but still perhaps a desire. Music is a universal language that is shared equally around the globe. I remember an international student from Korea coming to Canada, arriving with music books in hand to study with me. As I opened her books and said that I would play a few pieces for her to choose from, I could see her eyes getting bigger and bigger, and in her broken English she said, "Miss Glory, you speak Korean?" I wanted to impress her and say yes, but of course, I said no; however, I do speak the language of music, which is the same around the world. Her only friend, her music books, the one thing she held so dear to her heart, opened the door to a new relationship with me.

Musical relationships are a treasure to each and every one of us. Can you imagine a world without music? Me neither. I grew up in a musical family; my dad was a multi-instrumentalist playing guitar, piano, stand-up bass, organ, harmonica, banjo, you name it, he played it. He also sang in a gospel quartet. Music lessons in our home were like brushing your teeth – yes, you do it every day and more than once. My mother played the violin and at the age of sixty-five began accordion lessons - Why? Because my mother, Rosabel, loved music. She also knew that learning music makes you smarter – many scientific studies have been conducted researching how the consistent practice of music increases cognitive function in specific neurological areas. And my mother told me that teaching music makes you better looking, apparently another fact from my mother, yet to undergo scientific research.

When my mother was diagnosed with breast cancer, she could no longer play her accordion and so it remained in the case, which I still have to this day. I remember thinking about the musical sound an ambulance plays on its hurried way to save a life. A sound that scares you and gives you hope all at the same time. When my mother lay in the hospital bed for the last four days of her life, I stayed in the room with her, along with my daughter Sherry and best friend Laureen. She asked me to play some recordings of the music that she loved so dearly so she could hear uplifting songs that brought back memories of times when she played with *her orchestra* called the *Pembina Players*. She asked me to turn up the music louder so she could close her eyes and truly immerse herself in the memory of performing on stage with her beloved musicians.

The nurse came in and quietly said, "Your mother is dying, turn down the music."

I said, "My mother, is the one who told me to TURN IT UP!"

"Ah..." was her reply as she left quickly knowing the end for my mother would soon be here. My mother brought me into this world of music the day I was born and when she passed away and took her last breath, she left with the sound of music and to be with my dad, whose hummingbird guitar I treasure to this day. I felt alone but not lonely. The music seemed different. But the relationship of music that we shared, as I reflected on years gone by, as one often does at the time of a loved one passing, I remembered the lessons my mother taught me.

As I felt not good enough as a music teacher, she would simply smile and say, just watch as your students learn to fly and soar higher than you ever imagined. Memories are brought back through music. This symbol, the Treble Clef or G Clef (and now you know that stands for the Glory Clef), is a symbol of new beginnings. Each piece of music begins with a clef, just as each day begins with a sunrise. Each piece of music ends leaving you with a memory, just as each day ends with a sunset. Listen to the music, play, and create magic in your life.

May your relationship with music uplift you when you need to climb, heal you when you need to cry, and give you strength when you need to persevere, and ultimately bring you joy as you celebrate your life through the magic of musical relationships.

ACKNOWLEDGMENTS

There are many people I want to thank for being willing to share their ideas, their expertise, and ultimately their stories of inspiration, and most importantly their WHY.

Their WHY became the strategies that led them to their success. I am grateful to them and proud of them as they reveal the power of why their goals became a reality in this book.

I want to thank my 'UMT Dream Team' Shelagh McKibbon-U'Ren, Joanne Barker, Migs Luna, and Julie-Kristin Hardt who helped me to implement these ideas and share them with the world.

Thank you to the hundreds of musicians, entrepreneurs, teachers, and students that I have learned from through the years who gave me the framework to build my company, write the *Ultimate Music Theory Program, UMT Courses, UMT Membership*, and compile the *Power of Why - Musicians Series*.

Thank you to our editors Wendy H. Jones and Lisa McGrath for their guidance, expertise, and time in making this book possible.

It is with gratitude to everyone who has taken the risk to dream big and follow their heart to become a musician, an entrepreneur, and generously leave their legacy by enriching lives through music education.

These inspiring stories give you the "backstage pass" and off-the-record strategies of today's systems in creating high-profile techniques that you can apply to your music career with amazing results.

Thank you to the author-contributors, the ultimate "players" who have created a program, crafted a course, composed a legacy, capture the lead, and climbed to superstar status.

What's YOUR WHY to create, craft, compose, capture and climb as a musician?

ABOUT THE AUTHOR

Glory St. Germain ARCT RMT MYCC UMTC is the Founder/Author (50+ Books) of the *Ultimate Music Theory Program* and Founder of the *Magic of Music Movement*. She is on a mission to help 1 million teachers create a legacy through their business. She is the host of the *Global Music Teachers Summits*, Course Creator, Expert Music Teachers Coach, Publisher of the *Ultimate Music Theory Series*, and an International Bestselling Author in *The Power of Why Series* (an anthology of global authors).

She is the founder of the UMTC ELITE EDUCATOR PROGRAM - A Business Accelerator in knowledge and expert strategies for teachers to use in order to run their successful music studios. She empowers educators to elevate their income, impact their teaching, and build their expert music business while enjoying personal time for self-care, family, and pursuing other passions.

In addition Glory is an NLP Practitioner (Neuro-Linguistic Programming) and has taught Piano, Theory, and Music for Young Children for over 20 years. She has served in various leadership positions to support music education organizations. Glory has spoken on many international stages presenting workshops and is passionate about *Enriching Lives Through Music Education.*

Glory loves learning and especially loves books on business and psychology. Mindset is a subject she believes has the potential to change our outcomes. Mindset is limited only by our own thinking. She is a Positive Mental Attitude Advocate and *strongly believes* that we need to see mindset as a priority, not only for ourselves but also for how we help others think, learn, and grow.

She is married to Ray St. Germain, a professional *multi-award-winning* entertainer and Canadian Country Music Hall of Fame inductee. They have five musically talented children, many grandchildren, and the family continues to grow.

Glory lives her life with gratitude, passion, and serving others through her work.

https://UltimateMusicTheory.com

www.ingramcontent.com/pod-product-compliance
Lightning Source LLC
Chambersburg PA
CBHW061032050726
47592CB00004B/1410